🦇🦇🦇🦇🦇🦇 DIVING AND SNORKELING GUIDE TO 🦇🦇🦇🦇🦇🦇

Scotland

Lawson Wood

Pisces Books®
A division of Gulf Publishing Company
Houston, Texas

Pisces Books®
A division of Gulf Publishing Company
P.O. Box 2608
Houston, Texas 77252-2608

Pisces Books is a registered trademark of Gulf Publishing Company.

Printed in Hong Kong

10 9 8 7 6 5 4 3 2 1

Library of Congress Cataloging-in-Publication Data

Wood, Lawson.
    Diving and snorkeling guide to Scotland : includes Shetlands, Scapa Flow, and Hebrides / Lawson Wood.
        p.   cm.
    Includes bibliographical references (p.   ) and index.
    ISBN 1-55992-094-7
        1. Scuba diving—Scotland—Guidebooks.   2. Skin diving—Scotland—Guidebooks.   3. Scotland—Guidebooks.   I. Title.
    GV840.S78W66   1996
    797.2′3′09411—dc20   96-20581
                                                                          CIP

The photographs were taken using Nikonos 111, Nikonos 1VA, Nikonos V, Nikon F-801, Nikon F-90 and the Pentax LX. Lenses used on the amphibious Nikonos system were 35mm; 15mm; 12mm, and various extension tubes. The lenses for the housed Nikons and Pentax were 14mm; 50mm; 60mm; 105mm; 28-200mm zoom, and 70-300mm zoom. Housing manufacture is by Subal in Austria and Hugyphot in Switzerland.

Electronic flash was used in virtually all of the underwater photographs. These units were supplied by Sea & Sea Ltd. and included the YS20, YS50, YS200, and YS300. For the land cameras, the Nikon SB24 and SB26 were used. Film stock used was Fujichrome Velvia, Fujichrome Provia, Fujichrome RDP, and some Ektachrome.

Table of Contents

Submarine Pens, Loch Long, 77 • Catalina Seaplane, Cumbrae, Firth of Clyde, 78 • Ailsa Craig, 79

Acknowledgments

This book is somewhat of a culmination of more than thirty years of diving around Scottish shores. It is impossible to list all of the help I have received over the years, but there are some notable exceptions: John Reid of the *Jean De La Lune,* who finally got me out to St. Kilda; Gordon Ridley, whose diving exploration of the Scottish coastline is legendary and fuelled my interest so many years ago; The Royal Navy; Lt. Cdr. Chris Davies from The Royal Navy's Clearance Diving Unit, who arranged for my diving on one of the greatest shipwrecks of our time, H.M.S. *Royal Oak* in Scapa Flow; Joe Rocks and the Shetlands Islands Tourist Board; The Berwickshire Branch of the Scottish Sub Aqua Club, my local dive club; my main diving buddy, my wife Lesley, who unswervingly supports me and allows me to develop my passion for our underwater world; my granddaughter, Rebecca, who thinks I star in every underwater programme on the television!

How to Use This Guide

The locations described in this guide include some of the most popular regarding access, marine life, interest, location, and services available. The intention was not to write the definitive book on underwater Scotland, but rather a guide to some of the best dive sites that Scottish waters offer. (Although some may consider my choices to be rather arbitrary, I think my 30+ years of diving around Scotland allow me to present a fair sampling of the diversity of diving.) Scotland could quite easily be split up into three distinct areas, each with thousands of dive sites. The Scottish east coast, the Highlands and Islands, and the west coast sea lochs all have distinct ecosystems and all yield a rich variety of marine life, wrecks, and staggering scenery.

Wherever you are in Scotland, exploratory divers should always consult with the Admiralty Tidal Stream Atlas, ordinance survey maps, local coastguards in their diving area and if possible, collect accurate up-to-date information from local contacts such as dive stores or even other divers.

Dive Site and Skill Level Classification

Conventional rating systems are not really practical due to the great diversity of dive sites found around Scottish shores. Conditions do change during a dive, sudden currents can sweep in and a strong wind can whip the sea state into a dangerous condition. I have decided to split the diver skill level into three areas of expertise:

- #1 Beginner—Snorkellor or trainee diver with a minimum of skill.
- #2 Intermediate—Qualified diver but with less than 100 dives.
- #3 Advanced—Experienced diver under all conditions.

The dive site grading is on a similar basis:

- #1 Easy shore dive and snorkelling, little current.
- #2 Shallow reef dive from shore or boat, little to some current.
- #3 Deeper dive to offshore reef or wall, always current.
- #4 Deep dive to wreck or reef, and/or strong current.

Quite often the shallowest and easiest dive sites yield the highest rewards for marine life and just sheer enjoyment. Just because the dive site is listed as easy and dive skill level as beginner, there is no reason to think that it is beneath you. The dive sites chosen reflect a purely subjective choice where it is superb for photography, marine life, and overall good diving. You do not have to be a 'macho diver' to enjoy Scotland.

1

Overview of Scotland

Scotland is such a vast and diverse landscape, encompassing many islands, sea lochs and mountain scenery, that to illustrate and write a guide on the best diving sites in Scotland, one can only generalise. The diversity of marine life and the unspoiled scenery are just a small part of what is essentially Scotland.

The capital city of Edinburgh is a delight, and just over the Firth of Forth in North Queensferry, nestled under the famous Forth Bridge, is Deep Sea World, which is the largest saltwater aquarium in Europe, featuring Scottish marine life. The other major city is Glasgow, designated a European City of Culture. Dundee, Aberdeen, and Inverness all deserve further mention. The Highlands and Glens' history and folklore have carved a country with the oldest mountains in the world into a unique holiday destination that offers safe, exciting dive opportunities.

The island of Hirta in the St. Kilda Archipelago is Europe's most westerly inhabited island.

Deep Sea World Marine Aquarium in Fife is the largest of its kind in Europe to feature Scottish marine life.

Transportation

Although Scotland is large (for those who live there), distances are relatively small and if for some reason your diving is prohibited on the east coast due to inclement weather, it will only take you 2 to 3 hours to drive to the first of the sheltered sea lochs on the west coast. As you travel farther north, the roads tend to be more circuitous due to the rugged terrain, but you can still drive from the Scottish border to Scrabster in the extreme north of the Scottish mainland (where you catch the ferry to the Orkneys) in under six hours. Car hire (rental) is an obvious choice and all of the airports and ferry terminals have the usual Avis and Hertz.

Remember that when coming from overseas, driving is on the left side and that you will have to present a valid driver's licence. There are also excellent rail links between all the major towns, but the rail now travels no farther north than Inverness, where you will then have to travel by bus or hire (rent) car. The air link between the main international airports of Edinburgh and Glasgow connecting the smaller regional airports at Aberdeen, Inverness, Stornaway, Oban, Skye, Orkney, and Shetland is also regular and an hour's flight will get you almost anywhere.

Accommodations

Traditional bed and breakfast establishments are the order of the day in the Highlands and offer the most reasonable prices. Hotels are everywhere, of course, and prices will vary according to the range of facilities on offer. Scandanavian style log cabins, chalets, and caravan holiday homes are also an alternative and with perhaps six people sharing, the costs can work out extremely favourably. Many of the larger diving operations offer all-inclusive packages of accommodation, diving, food, boat hire, etc. For a com-

3

Eyemouth Harbour on the Scotland's southeast coast is a popular destination for divers.

Scottish pipers seen here playing on Princes Street in the Scottish capital of Edinburgh.

prehensive list of accommodations in the area that you are visiting, contact the Scottish Tourist Board, 23 Ravelston Terrace, Edinburgh, Scotland. EH4; tel: (00 44) 131 332 2433; fax: (00 44) 131 343 1513.

The Scottish Tourist Board will put you in touch with the other regional offices and will also book your hotels in advance for you. They offer a superb service and should not be ignored.

Foreign Exchange, Dining, and Shopping

Scotland is part of the British Isles and although the Scottish independent identity is fiercely defended, British currency is used throughout. Coins come in 5p, 10p, 20p, 50p, £1, and £2 denominations. Notes are £1, £5, £10, £20, £50 and £100 in value.

It should be noted that the Scottish £1 note, although legal tender is generally not accepted in England.

Currently, the exchange rate fluctuates around 1.5 U.S. dollars equaling 1 pound sterling. All of the banks, post offices, and buereau de Change offer the same rates. For those travelling from overseas, as always, currency is often better in travellers' cheques, and credit cards are accepted everywhere. Crime is not really a problem in Scotland, but, care should always be taken with your personal possessions.

Scotland is world renowned for the 'water of life', and the number of whiskey distilleries and variety of flavours are a whisky connoisseur's dream. Traditional recipes of shortbread biscuits travel the globe and the greatest ambassador of all is the kilt. Those with Scottish lineage are entitled to wear the kilt that bears their family name, and the tartan designs worn by the Scottish Pipers are splendid. Local crafts of semi-precious stones and silver in Celtic designs are another favourite and what self-respecting gentleman could visit without owning a Harris Tweed jacket?

Dining out has changed somewhat over the years; we do not all eat haggis in Scotland and the cuisine is now to international standards. Many small restaurants serve the more traditional Scottish dishes, but perhaps the beef, lamb, and salmon are most worthy of note. Seafood features very highly and is always fresh. Small villages all have the traditional fish & chip shops, where your take-away meal is still served in newspaper!

Besides diving, Scotland is the home of golf and the Old Course at St. Andrews is world famous. Other top-class golf courses include Gleneagles, Royal Troon, and Muirfield. The walking and hiking in the Highlands is excellent and 'Munro Bagging' is the ultimate. Skiing in Glen Shee and salmon fishing on the River Tweed and Royal Dee are what legends are made of. Some of the most secluded and whitest sand beaches in the world are found in the Outer Hebrides and films such as *Rob Roy; Braveheart,* and *Whisky Galore* have depicted our glorious and inglorious past.

There are many national nature reserves; those and historical homes and castles are always a delight and well worth a visit. Information can be obtained from:

The National Trust for Scotland, 5 Charlotte Square, Edinburgh
Tel: (00 44) 131 226 5922 Fax: (00 44) 131 243 9302

Scottish Battlefield & Historic Tours, 28 North Bridge, Edinburgh
Tel: (00 44) 0131 226 2202; Fax: (00 44) 0131 226 2818

Scottish Wildlife Trust, Cramond House, Cramond Glebe Rd. Edinburgh.
  EH4 6NS
Tel: (00 44) 0131 312 7765; Fax: (00 44) 0131 312 8705

Scottish Natural Heritage, Battleby, Redgorton, Perthshire. PH1 3EW
Tel: (00 44) 01738 627 921; Fax: (00 44) 01738 630 583

Association of Scottish Visitor Attractions
4 Rothesay Terrace, Edinburgh. EH3
Tel: (00 44) 0131 555 2551; Fax: (00 44) 0131 555 2552

2

Diving in Scotland

The entire length of the Scottish coastline including all of the islands and sea lochs is more than 6,500 miles (10,500 km), which is equivalent to travelling from Scotland to Japan! Given these facts, it is not surprising that Scotland not only yields a vast number of dive locations, there is also virtually every underwater ecosystem to be found around this rugged and varied land. Diving Scotland's coastline can be an exhilarating experience, the underwater life is exceptionally profuse, there are many exciting wrecks, and the underwater cliffs and caves are tremendous. There is an almost total lack of 'diver pollution', except at one or two of the southern sites and then again, only during peak holiday time.

Those specific locations may suffer from 'diver pollution', but that is because of the infrastructure available. Their facilities include road and rail link; accommodations of various types and standard; equipment sales and hire; boat hire; launching facilities; compressors; instruction; wrecks; photography; marine reserves etc.

A diver explores a submarine wall covered in soft corals.

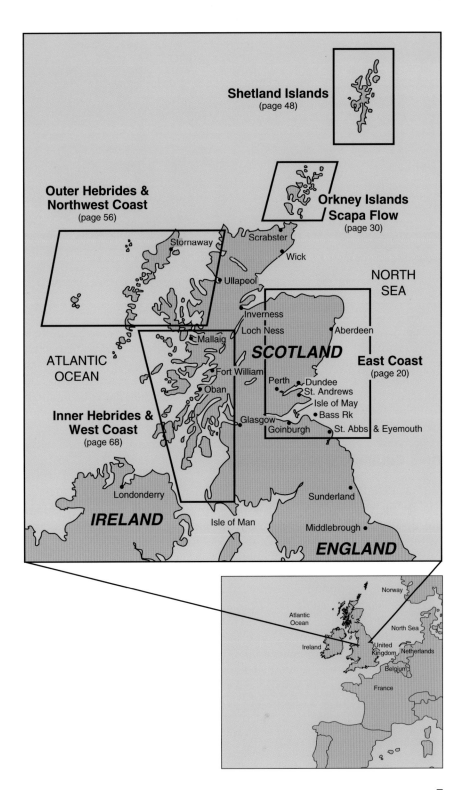

Shetland Islands
(page 48)

Outer Hebrides &
Northwest Coast
(page 56)

Orkney Islands
Scapa Flow
(page 30)

Scrabster

Stornaway

Wick

Ullapool

NORTH
SEA

Inverness

Loch Ness

Aberdeen

SCOTLAND

ATLANTIC
OCEAN

Mallaig

East Coast
(page 20)

Fort William

Perth

Dundee

Oban

St. Andrews

Isle of May

Inner Hebrides &
West Coast
(page 68)

Glasgow

Bass Rk

Goinburgh

St. Abbs & Eyemouth

Londonderry

Sunderland

IRELAND

Isle of Man

Middlebrough

ENGLAND

Norway

Atlantic
Ocean

North Sea

Ireland

United
Kingdom

Netherlands

Belgium

France

7

Swimming amongst the kelp forest on the Scottish east coast is always a delight.

A diver climbs aboard the Scapa Flow dive boat M.V. Triton after another successful deep dive on the sunken German Fleet. ▶

The dives range from those easy, gently sloping shore dives to challenging drift dives in difficult tidal conditions. There are little-dived major wrecks, and many undiscovered wreck sites enticingly marked on the Admiralty Charts. Finally, there are mind-blowing underwater caves and tunnels, and breathtaking dives on vertical overhanging underwater cliffs. Some of these cliffs extend well below the safe air diving range, and thus are effectively 'bottomless.'

Dive Equipment and Training

It is essential to remember that when diving the more remote offshore islands, there will be very little back-up if there should be equipment failure of any type. It is therefore best to aim for complete independence within your diving group. All of the boat charter operators have air cylinders, compressor, weights, etc., but there is very little of any other equipment available. Divers should bring dry suits, thermal undersuits, water and wind-proof clothing, spare parts for gear if necessary, and battery rechargers etc. that can operate from a ship's in-board electrical system. If you wear prescription lenses in a customised mask, then take a spare if you can. It is also common sense to carry a good first-aid kit, together with instructions on how to use it.

Much of the diving in Scottish waters is a serious undertaking and it is assumed that most readers will have a full working knowledge of decompression tables, the use of a tidal stream atlas, and tide tables; however, many of the dive centres offer instruction and several are PADI Five Star Centres, offering the full range of training. All are available to offer advice on any dive location. Open-water divers should have a minimum of safety equipment always on their person, such as day-glow hood, emergency

Wherever the water is particularly clear, the kelp grows much deeper, shown here as this diver passes over the kelp in the Shetland Islands.

strobe light, surface marker bouy or mini-flares. There can be a very real danger of being swept out to sea in a strong current.

Wreck divers should be aware of the dangers of snagging equipment and never enter a wreck without the proper training and a safety line. Diving along drop-offs has the additional danger of extreme depth and limited available time. Careful bouyancy control is essential.

Tunnel diving requires little extra instruction other than an awareness of the power of oceanic surge, which can hurtle you through a hole or dash you just as easily into the rocks. Drift diving is always exhilarating and again be certain that the boat cover is aware of your position by the use of a surface marker bouy.

Much of the deeper wreck diving involves decompression diving to some level and only the most experienced of divers should undertake this type of diving. Much of the diving is also far away from any emergency medical services and great care should be taken at all times. It is essential that dive boats carry ship-to-shore radio and oxygen on board.

Diving in Scottish waters can be challenging, but most of all it is exciting, packed with marine life, and within sight of some of the most outstanding mountain scenery of Europe. These facts, plus the remoteness, considerably heighten any experience you may have.

Wind and Water Conditions

Water visibility varies drastically along the Scottish east coast and is affected by the prevailing wind. There are no strong tidal streams, so sedimentation occurs after a prolonged on-shore wind from the North Sea. Unfortunately, these on-shore winds can result in the entire east coast

This pincushion starfish (Porania pulvillus *) is commonly found on the west coast and northern islands; it is quite small and always brightly coloured.*

being too rough and dangerous for any type of diving. The west coast however, has huge sheltered sea lochs and fjords that offer protection from any strong winds and leave the water fairly calm all year round and certainly diveable. Visibility in these sea lochs tends to be less than around the outer islands because there is less water movement and more surface sedimentation from the rain water run-off from the hills. There are also no strong currents to speak of except at the entrances to these long narrow lochs, where there is perhaps a restriction or rocky outcrops above and below water. The Falls of Lora (Dive Site No. 24) is one such area.

The outer islands are more susceptible to offshore winds and of course the might of the Atlantic swell and tidal range. Visibility is always better and the water invariably has that 'blue' quality. Tidal variations and current can be punishing to say the least. The Gulf of Corryvrecken is world renowned for the spectacular whirlpool that forms when converging currents reach more than 8 knots, running from opposite directions, and meet over a submarine peak that rises from 660 ft (200 m) to just 100 ft (30 m). Slack water is only 10 minutes during spring tides.

As you travel north to the Orkney Islands, most of the diving occurs in Scapa Flow. This is deep diving, on the remains of the German Battle Fleet, which was scuttled in 1919. There is now a technical diving operation for those qualified with mixed gas. The visibility in Scapa Flow at depth is always poor due to the lack of water movement to clear away any

St. Abbs harbour on the southeast coast is a favourite site for boat launching to dive the St. Abbs & Eyemouth Voluntary Marine Nature Reserve.

sedimentation. The entrances to Scapa are much better as clear Atlantic water runs through.

The most northerly reaches of Scotland around the Shetland Islands are exceptional, visibility is always good and the marine life prolific. Temperatures around the coastline are variable, but the general rule is that the west coast is warmer due to the far-reaching effect of the Gulf Stream.

The mean sea temperatures are 46°F (7.5°C) in February, 48°F (9°C) in May, 65°F (18°C) in August and 51°F (10.5°C) in November. Temperatures are cold, and visiting divers should make certain that they have proper thermal semi-dry or dry suits. In every dive, cold is the limiting factor. Wind chill must also be considered. A good quality wet suit may be ideal underwater, but the problems relating to wind chill on leaving the water are commonplace and hypothermia can result from a long boat journey after the dives, whilst sitting in cold, wet gear.

Tidal streams and currents are much stronger on the west coast, particularly around some of the inner islands, and a tidal atlas should be consulted before venturing into these waters. However, most charter boat skippers are all very experienced in these waters and the utmost care is always taken.

Highlights of Scottish Diving

Visitors to Scotland arrive by three means, either by flying in to the two major airports of Edinburgh or Glasgow (and connecting other flights to the Outer Hebrides, Orkney, and Shetland); or by ferry. The Scandanavian

Mavis Grind in the Shetland Islands is a narrow strip of land that separates the Atlantic Ocean from the North Sea.

ferries dock at Leith in Edinburgh and Newcastle upon Tyne. The closest car ferry terminal from Europe is Hull, just 4 hours' drive from the Scottish border where the first and one of the best diving locations can be located—Eyemouth (Dive Site Nos. 1 and 2). Your first port of call is also one of the best dive locations in the entire British Isles—the St. Abbs and Eyemouth Voluntary Marine Nature Reserve, just 7 miles (11 km) north of the Scottish border. The marine reserve runs from the Hurkar Rocks at Eyemouth and stretches to St. Abbs Head. Its 4½-mile (7 km) coastline reaches out to the 165-ft-depth contour (50m).

This is still the only voluntary marine reserve in Scotland and has long been established as the ideal site for all standards of diver. In fact, those who are fortunate enough to dive here for the first time will never forget the experience. The Nature Conservancy Council (now Scottish Heritage) and the Marine Conservation Society both list the area as probably the best shore diving site in the entire British Isles. There is also a National Nature Reserve at St. Abbs Head where you can find the largest number of breeding seabirds anywhere on mainland Britain, and during May and June you can dive underwater with guillemots, razorbills, puffins, and shags!

A wide variety of marine ecosystems can be found on this 4½-mile (7-km) stretch of coastline with its clean unpolluted water. There are wrecks (though mainly broken up); cliff faces festooned with dead mens' fingers (soft corals), anemones, hydroids, and nudibranchs; large boulder-strewn areas where ballan wrasse eat out of your hand and wolffish try to eat your hand; and kelp forests with sea urchins, spider crabs, two-spot blennies, and brittlestar beds with giant dahlia and plumose anemones, and huge anglerfish. Octopus and squid are common on night dives and the rare yarrel's blenny isn't rare here amongst the gulleys, canyons, and caves that cut through the underwater headlands.

On the west coast of Scotland the other main centre is Oban in Argyllshire. Oban is your gateway to the Inner and Outer Hebrides. The Sound of Mull is one of the most famous areas, having 10 spectacular wrecks, each with a varied history dating from the 16th century to modern times. Probably the two most famous are the *Hispania* and the *Rondo*.

The *Hispania,* a Swedish merchant vessel 265 ft (81 m) long and completely intact in 100 ft (30 m) of water, is smothered in marine life (Dive Site No. 23). The *Rondo* at 250 ft (76 m) in length was a Norwegian tramp steamer and sits on a near vertical slope. The rudder post is a mere 3 m below the surface because she came to rest in soft mud in 180 ft (55 m) of water. All of the Oban wrecks are affected by strong tidal streams, so care must be taken.

The lesser octopus (Eledone cirrhosa*) is the most common of the octopus species found around Scotland. Quite small in size, it is an active predator at night.*

The diver serves as a suitable 'measuring stick' to show the size of this anglerfish.

By booking on to one of the capable charter boats (see Appendix), you can extend your diving range to the Inner Hebrides of Mull, Iona, Coll, Muck, Rhum, Eigg, Skye, and Canna. All of these islands offer spectacular and sheltered diving, but by far the best is to sail out beyond the protective barrier of the Outer Hebrides and sail to the Flannan Islands and the St. Kilda Archipelago.

The St. Kilda Archipelago is situated 35 miles (55 km) westnorthwest of the Island of North Uist. These are the most exciting landforms in the British Isles and rise more than 1,500 feet (500 m) from the seabed. The jagged tooth of Am Plastair is cut by a tunnel which leads all the way through, and the finest underwater arch on the west coast can be found at Sgarbhstac to the southwest of Boreray. The main island of Hirta has a huge sheltered bay and spectacular night dives can be had in the Sawcut (Dive Site No. 16).

The isle of Skye has another equally famous wreck, the *Port Napier* at 9,600 tons and 330 ft (100 m) long and resting in 66 ft (20 m) of water. The lack of appreciable current makes this one of the most desirable photographic wrecks. *The Port Napier* is situated in the sheltered bay of Loch Alsh and still has her cargo of mines and ammunition.

I think it only fair to point out that many of the potential dives on the west coast are to be regarded as *very serious* undertakings. Drift dives in exposed and remote situations demand the utmost care and preplanning.

However, it is also easy to say that there are many wonderful dives on the west coast in areas sheltered from tides and weather. The Summer Isles are one such location. This large group of 30 small islands covers an area of 5 mi^2 (8 km^2) and is largely uninhabited. Seals abound in the waters, and dolphins and porpoises are spotted regularly. The tidal streams are generally weak and the underwater visibility is nearly always in the 66-ft (20-m)

Yarrell's blenny (Chiropholis ascanii), *a smaller relative of the wolffish at only 8 in. (20 cm), is considered rare in Scotland.*

The dive boat Jean de la Lune *is seen here leaving St. Kilda and making towards the Flannan Islands.*

range. Marine life includes jewel anemones, scallops, sea pens, and squat lobsters. There are also several wrecks in the area, one of which is reputed to be a Spanish Armada ship that foundered off Horse Island.

The north coast from Cape Wrath to John O' Groats is spectacularly rugged and diving must be well planned due to the adversity of the weather and structure of the land itself. The northern islands of the Orkneys and Shetlands group also yield some of the most spectacular diving in the British Isles. It is true to say that of Scotland's 747 islands the Orkneys and Shetlands rate very highly indeed.

Scapa Flow in Orkney is justifiably famous for the sinking of the German Fleet in 1919, and has the largest concentration of shipwrecks in the world. The diving on these ancient battleships is both eerie and spectacular, but unfortunately many of the wrecks are in very deep water. The best wreck photography can be found around the 'blockships', which in many cases are only partially submerged and make superb photographic subjects.

All around Scotland you will find sheltered bays and inlets, sleepy harbours and generally good diving, with a wide range of accommodations available, but you can still waste time if you do not know specifically where to go. The best bet for diving in Scotland is to book into one or several of the dive centres perhaps Eyemouth, Oban, Stromness, or Skye. This would give the widest range of habitats, wrecks, and dive sites available. Charter boats are of course ideal, and there is a wide range of liveaboards and day boats.

A Highland pond covered in lilies can also make an interesting freshwater dive.

I would be remiss if I did not mention the **freshwater diving** in Scotland. All of the lochs are accessible, but very deep, silty, and rather dull. However, on the other hand, diving in the rivers and deep pools is absolutely superb. Glen Etive, for instance, has very clear water, and there is a good chance to encounter trout and salmon as they swim upstream to the spawning grounds. Similarly, the River Tweed near Kelso in the Scottish Borders has some deep pools that are also very interesting. Scotland is for the exploratory diver, so try the rivers, too. You will not be disappointed and remember to check with the local Tourist Board to see if special permission is required, particularly during the fishing season.

Loch Ness is the deepest Loch in Scotland and home to the fabled Loch Ness Monster. Many searches have been undertaken to prove or disprove the existance of the 'monster', and you can actually dive in a submersible that takes four passengers plus the pilot to depths of 600 ft (180 m) and more, in relative comfort. This deepwater submersible is situated near Urquart Castle on the shores of Loch Ness, where 'Nessie' was first spotted.

The waters in Loch Ness are peaty brown in colour, and undertaking an assignment to photograph the submersible as she sank into the depths with me on the outside, I could not help but wonder about what was swimming below in the murky depths. The seashore slopes steeply away over a jumble

Urquart Castle on the shore of Loch Ness is near where the Loch Ness 'monster' was first spotted.

of rocks and ancient tree stumps. Small fish are attracted to the lights of the submersible, but nothing larger was prepared to show itself that day !

Marine Conservation in Scotland

All of the marine areas and coastline around Scotland come under the jurisdiction of Scottish National Heritage. There are, as yet, no statutory marine reserves and only one fully operational voluntary reserve. The St. Abbs and Eyemouth Voluntary Marine Nature Reserve is the first and only one of its kind in Scotland. Situated on the southeast coast of Scotland, the reserve is being extended to be the largest of its kind in Europe with a multimillion-pound investment to construct an interpretive and interactive centre. The marine reserve already employs a full-time warden who undertakes school education classes, marine biology courses, etc.

Marine conservation is still in its infancy in the British Isles, but there are many local groups and diving clubs affiliated with the Marine Conservation Society. For information on local groups and expeditions taking place around Scotland, which you can become part of, please contact:

The Conservation Officer
Marine Conservation Society
9 Gloucester Road, Ross-on-Wye
Tel: (44) 01989 566017

The castle is now the home base of a more practical monster—the Loch Ness submarine. As it descends into the murky, peat-coloured waters of Scotland's deepest loch, does 'Nessie' await?

Diving Along the East Coast

Started in 1978, the St. Abbs and Eyemouth Voluntary Marine Nature Reserve on the southeast coast of Scotland is still the only marine reserve in the country. The rugged shoreline is home to some of the greatest diversity of marine life to be found around Scotland. Tidal currents from both the warm Gulf Stream and the much colder Arctic Tidal Stream both terminate along this stretch of coastline and create an area of clear, clean water where arctic species are found living alongside more exotic west coast species.

East Coast Dive Sites	Skill Level			Site Rating			
	Beginner	Intermediate	Advanced	1	2	3	4
1. Weasal Loch	x	x	x	x	x		
2. Fold Buss		x	x			x	x
3. Cathedral Rock	x	x	x		x		
4. Tye's Tunnel		x	x			x	x
5. Dunbar	x	x	x	x	x		
6. Bass Rock		x	x			x	x
7. Isle of May		x	x			x	x
8. Catterline	x	x	x		x		
9. Castle Point, Portsoy	x	x	x	x	x		

Dive site ratings:

1—Easy shore dive and snorkelling, little current
2—Shallow reef dive from shore or boat, little to mild current
3—Deeper dive to offshore reef or wall, always current
4—Deep dive to wreck or reef, and/or strong current

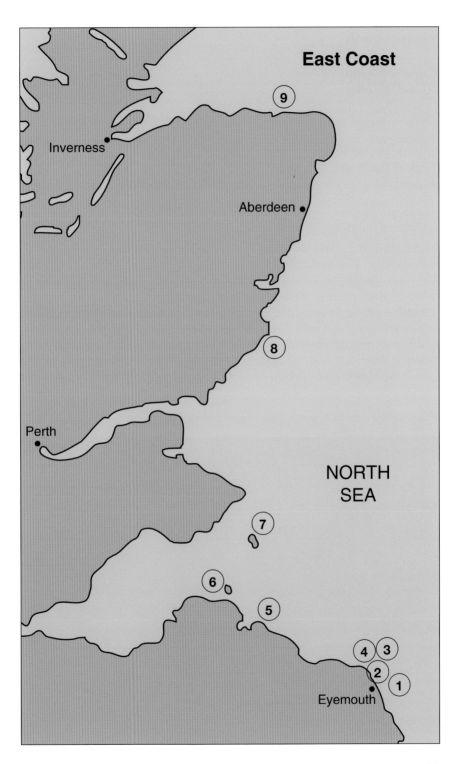

East Coast

⑨

Inverness •

Aberdeen •

⑧

Perth •

NORTH
SEA

⑦

⑥

⑤

④ ③

②

①

Eyemouth •

Expertise Required:	1
Overall Grade:	1–2
Location:	Shore dive off the Caravan Holiday Home Park in Eyemouth, Berwickshire, S.E. Coast.
Typical Depth Range:	10–40 ft (3–12 m)
Typical Current Conditions:	Nil to slight
Access:	Directly from the shore.

This is one of the dives within the boundaries of the St. Abbs and Eyemouth Voluntary Marine Nature Reserve (see page 19). The cliff is about 65 ft high (20 m) and there are sturdy wooden steps leading down to the water's edge. This vertical cleft cut into the rugged Berwickshire coastline has walls lined with kelp (*Laminaria hyperborea*), and the sandy floor is home to all manner of molluscs and crustaceans.

Farther round to the right, the mini-wall is covered in soft corals and numerous species of anemone. The kelp forest reaches to only 25 ft (8 m) in this area and the far wall is deeply undercut with some very large holes where conger eels and wolffish can be found. The wolffish (*Anarhichas lupus*) has quite a reputation for eating crabs and lobster with its large

This diver is exploring a narrow gully fringed with kelp.

*Wolffish (*Anarhichas lupus*), one of the few arctic species of fish found along the Scottish east coast, here showing its tongue and interlocking large front teeth.*

interlocking front teeth. A relation of the more common blenny, the wolf-fish can grow to more than 5 ft in length (1.5 m). Octopi are always found along this stretch of coast and during the full moon squid come close to shore to lay their large gelatinous eggs amongst the kelp fronds.

Swimming crabs can be found all over the sandy areas as well as small flounders, shrimps, and necklace shells (*Natica catena*). Nudibranchs are also a major feature of this area, although there are seasonal changes, more than 50 species have been recorded from this area alone. If this is your first time in Scotland, this is a superb dive for all levels, but you should call in advance to check the weather and sea conditions, because if the weather is bad, it can be horrendous here and you will not even be able to enter the water. When all is well, this location is also excellent for snorkelling and for introducing you to the pleasures of night diving.

Expertise Required:	2
Overall Grade:	3–4
Location:	Offshore dive between Eyemouth and St. Abbs along the outer edge of Coldingham Bay, Berwickshire
Typical Depth Range:	33–100 ft (10–30 m)
Typical Current Conditions:	Moderate to strong
Access:	By dive boat only

This is a difficult offshore site near the main shipping lane for boats entering Eyemouth harbour from the north. It is a long rocky ridge that stretches for several miles and has numerous submarine peaks. There is always a current in this area and you should have good boat cover and diver recovery flags, because the sea swell can be quite high and it may be difficult to see the boat under the worst conditions.

A narrow gulley encrusted in soft corals (Alcyonium digitatum) commonly known as 'dead men's fingers'.

The Bolocera anemone is an arctic species found in deeper water along the Scottish east coast. They are able to shed their tentacles when danger approaches.

The reef, although low-lying, has many mini-walls, underhangs, and crevices. They are completely covered in soft corals (*Alcyonium digitatum*) of two colour varieties and some huge arctic species of anemones called *Bolocera*. One of the many varieties of shrimp lives under the protective embrace of the anemone's tentacles. Common lobster, edible crabs, and wolffish can be found on every dive. Bottle brush hydroids dot the rocky outcrops and tiny crustaceans and molluscs are everywhere.

To the northern edge of this reef are the remains of a German U-Boat, but the seabed is made up of soft shale, so it moves around and is often completely covered, making it impossible to find. The reef once more surfaces near St.Abbs and breaks the surface at low tide. This section is called the Ebb Carrs and has two wrecks, the *Vigilant* and the *Alfred Earlandson*. Diving all along this area is indeed spectacular, but care should be taken due to boat traffic and the possibility of being swept into a stronger current than originally anticipated. Consult local tide tables available from the Coastguard, who also will be able to advise you of the best time to dive and when slack water is. The local dive centres also have excellent local knowledge.

Cathedral Rock   3

Expertise Required:	1
Overall Grade:	2
Location:	Shore and boat dive south of St. Abbs Harbour, Berwickshire
Typical Depth Range:	25–45 ft (8–14 m)
Typical Current Conditions:	Slight to moderate
Access:	Directly from the shore but can be done by boat (if you really insist!)

This is one of the most popular dive sites, and possibly one of the most dived in the whole of the British Isles. First discovered in the 1950s, this huge underwater archway has a smaller arch over it known locally as the Keyhole. This is an excellent dive and is diveable in any state of tide.

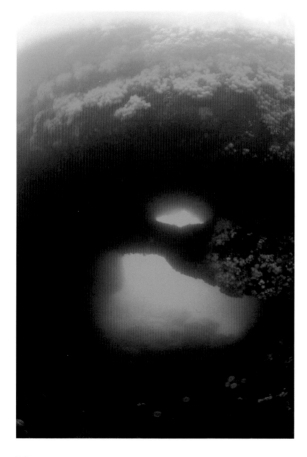

Cathedral Rock near St. Abbs Harbour is a popular location for people with different levels of expertise. This extreme wide-angle photograph shows the two archways, which are more than 30 ft across (9 m).

*Plumose anemones (*Metridium senile*) are common all around Scotland's coastline and are generally found in areas of moving water because they are plankton feeders.*

The best access is from the southern side of the harbour wall where it joins a low rocky reef. Directly opposite the entry point is another huge rock called Big Green Carr, which offers shelter except in the most exceptional of circumstances.

Drop down to 20 ft (6 m) onto the small sand patch, then swim over to the facing, almost vertical wall, follow it, keeping it to your left, and travel on as far as you can go. Then cross over a small headland that juts out from the right, swim straight on to the next facing wall, and by keeping it to your right you will come to Cathedral Rock. It is a swim of no more than 500 ft (150 m) and affords excellent marine life watching. After diving around the archway, work your way back slowly, thus enjoying the entire area.

Visibility is variable, depending on the prevailing winds, but is generally good. The walls and the roof of the arch are festooned in a dwarf species of the plumose anemone (*Metridium senile*) as well as sponges, soft corals, mussels, and hydroids. There is a resident family of ballan wrasse that will feed out of the divers' hands. This whole area is still part of the marine reserve and divers are discouraged to feed the fish with any of the local sea urchins. Why kill another animal to perhaps try and get better pictures? Please obey the conservation code; you will be amply rewarded.

Expertise Required:	2
Overall Grade:	3–4
Location:	Directly under St. Abbs lighthouse and just before you turn the corner into Pettycowick Bay, Berwickshire
Typical Depth Range:	20–66 ft (6–20 m)
Typical Current Conditions:	None in the tunnel, but can be subject to surge. Once you round the outer headland there will be moderate to strong current depending on tidal conditions.
Access:	By boat only

This is a superb dive site and just one of many to be found beneath the cliffs of this National Nature Reserve where hundreds of thousands of seabirds nest each year.

Boat launching is typically from either St. Abbs harbour or from Eyemouth farther to the south. Travel time tends to take around 20 minutes to reach St. Abbs Lighthouse. Directly opposite the entrance to the tunnel is

This diver has just emerged from a canyon totally smothered in soft corals and anemones, very much a feature of all Scottish diving.

*Short-spined scorpionfish (*Myoxocephalus scorpius*) are quite common all round the coast and are active predators, eating small shrimp and fish. They are also able to change colour like a chameleon.*

a huge rock called Cleaver Rock, which is underneath the lighthouse some 100 ft above (30 m). A narrow shaft 'bells out' as you descend and the tunnel bisects the headland. There have been numerous land-falls during the years and huge blocks of stone have fallen into the tunnel. These are easily negotiated and you will be able to swim completely through to the other side into a sheltered bay. The walls of the tunnel are completely covered in Dendrodoa sea squirts, small and red in colour as well as a type of bryozoan called *Clathrina,* which is white. Even the scorpionfish come in shades of red and white.

As you venture out to the headland past some huge boulders covered in soft corals, there is a small area of flat seabed, then the shelf drops away in 'fingers' similar to a spur and groove reef. On the tops and sides of the ridges, huge plumose anemones can be found in three colour varieties as well as thousands of brittle starfish. In the valleys between, some of the largest dahlia anemones I have ever seen can be found, as well as anglerfish (*Lophius piscatorius*) and the angel shark (*Squatina squatina*). There is more current in this area, and you should return the same way as you entered, seeking shelter from the current in the narrow grooves between the ridges.

Expertise Required:	1
Overall Grade:	1–2
Location:	Directly from the eastern side of the entrance to the harbour at Dunbar
Typical Depth Range:	10–45 ft (3–14 m)
Typical Current Conditions:	Slight with surge to be expected
Access:	Directly from the shore

This is a relatively easy dive and typical of the Scottish east coast shallow diving. Ideal for snorkelling and trainees, it is favoured by several diving schools as a great introduction to diving. Entry is from the shore to the right side of the entrance to Dunbar harbour.

The natural rock formations are incorporated into the harbour wall and shelve out to another reef that runs parallel to the shore. This is predominantly kelp and because of the huge boulders that make up much of the seabed, you are able to weave your way around these stacks, which are topped with kelp.

Octopus are seen regularly and, because it is quite sheltered, the site is also great for night dives. Diver's torches seem to illuminate the blue stripes on the squat lobsters as well as pick out all the colours on the dahlia anemones. Small wrasse follow you around after tidbits, and there are numerous large crabs and lobster. Although this is not a registered area of conservation, the local dive clubs that visit this site regularly have created a voluntary ban on the removal of any shellfish.

The squat lobster (Galathea strigosa) is perhaps the most strikingly coloured of all the marine crustaceans. The vivid blue stripes on the body can be seen more clearly with the use of underwater lights.

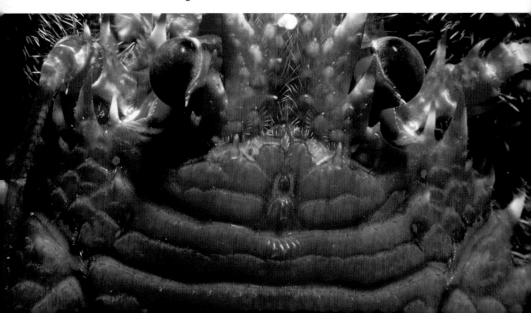

Expertise Required:	2
Overall Grade:	3–4
Location:	East of North Berwick and at the outer entrance to the Firth of Forth
Typical Depth Range:	10–100 ft (3–30 m)
Typical Current Conditions:	Slight to moderate with surge to be expected
Access:	By boat only

Bass Rock is a gigantic volcanic plug formed at the same time as the rock surrounding Edinburgh Castle. Rising vertically more than 200 ft (60 m) from the seabed, the vertical sides are just alive with all manner of sealife.

Topped with a fringe of kelp that extends down to 40 (12 m), ft in some areas seals dive past and harass the divers, generally moving too fast to take a picture. The small tunnel that cuts the rock at the western point is where many pups are born. The wall to the north of this tunnel is cut with numerous narrow fissures where butterfish (*Pholis gunnellus*) can be

*Butterfish (*Pholis gunellus), *though quite common in shallow water, are difficult to appoach. These eel-like fish grow as big as 5 in. (13 cm).*

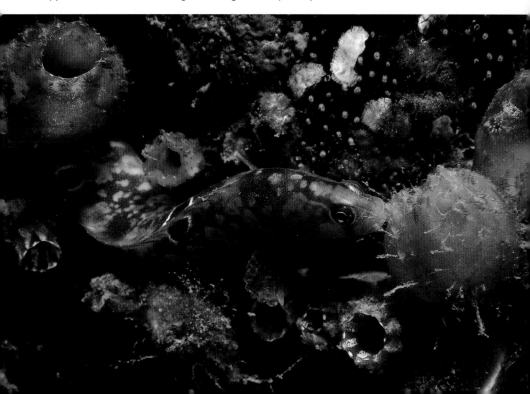

*The leopard-spotted goby (*Thorogobius ephippiatus*) was once considered very rare on the Scottish east coast. Now it is seen on most dives, standing on sentry duty outside its lair.*

found as well as the lesser octopus (*Eledone cirrhosa*). Look out for leopard-spotted gobies in the clefts; once considered rare in this stretch of coastline, they are quite common on Bass Rock.

The massive white cliffs of the rock can be seen for many miles. The white colour is the guano from the largest population of breeding gannets in the British Isles and are protected by law. These birds may fly as far as the Farne Islands 50 miles (80 km) to the south in the search for food once the chicks have hatched.

Access to the rock is by inflatable craft from either Dunbar harbour to the south or North Berwick to the west. The travel time is about the same and will take around 45 minutes. The sea can be rather choppy in this area as the major tidal flow from the Forth cuts between Bass Rock and the shore. It is always best to bring warm clothing to wear after the dive to prevent wind chill.

Expertise Required:	2
Overall Grade:	3–4
Location:	At the entrance to the Firth of Forth 6½ miles (10 km) south of Anstruther on the Fife coast
Typical Depth Range:	10–100 ft (3–30 m)
Typical Current Conditions:	Moderate to strong as well as surge
Access:	By boat only

This narrow island in the straits of the Firth of Forth covers 126 acres and is one of the main centres for recording the spring and autumn bird migrations. In fact there are probably more bird watchers than birds during May of each year. Like many Scottish Islands, the Isle of May attracted the early Christian missionaries, and St. Adrian was murdered on the island in the 9th century by raiders from Denmark.

The island provides excellent diving, but it is quite tidal, being at the confluence to the mouth of the River Forth, which virtually bisects Scotland, and the might of the North Sea. Surge conditions are always a problem and local knowledge of the tides and sea state should always be

This nudibranch (Polycera quadrilineata) is very common all around Scotland. Although seasonal, it is very distinguishable in its colouration and is often found in large groups.

*The tiny Atlantic cuttlefish (*Sepiola atlantica*) is only 1 in. long (3 cm).*

sought before venturing out to the island. Boat launching is usually from Anstruther or Pittenweem, both on the south shores of the Fife coastline.

Numerous wrecks dot the island's shoreline, particularly on the eastern face where it is fairly rugged and shallow. The remains of wreckage can also be found all over the place as you travel to the western edge of the island, where you will find that it is built up of huge tumbled rocks that form stepping stones into the depths. There are at least six well documented wrecks on the island as well as numerous others in much deeper water offshore.

Hundreds of gulleys and canyons are home to lobster, crabs, and schools of wrasse. In the more current-swept areas, fields of plumose anemones all stretch their tentacles out into the current. Cuttlefish and squat lobsters are common, as well as many species of nudibranch and shrimp.

Visibility is variable due to the amount of fresh water sedimentation that can flow down the Forth after some severe winter storms. During the summer months and on an in-coming tide, the diving can be excellent and well worth the effort of spending the whole day there, perhaps exploring the island and visiting the lighthouse and remains of the 13th century chapel.

Catterline 8

Expertise Required:	1
Overall Grade:	2
Location:	45 mi (75 km) north of Dundee and just off the A92 coastal road to Catterline Bay on the Scottish east coast
Typical Depth Range:	25–52 ft (8–16 m)
Typical Current Conditions:	Slight
Access:	By small inflatable or directly from the shore

Between Dundee and Aberdeen, Catterline Bay is probably one of the most popular dive locations north of the Firth of Forth. This shallow bay is shielded from the worst of the North Sea storms by a protective barrier of rocks forming a shallow reef. There is a broad shingle slope into the water, where it is possible to launch an inflatable boat; alternatively, many divers launch their boats a short distance away at Stonehaven harbour where there are three slipways, extensive facilities, and lots of parking.

The surrounding mini-wall from the southern edge of the bay is topped by 5 m or so of kelp forest with all the associated forms of marine life. The

The scampi prawn or Norway lobster (Nephrops norvegicus*) is considered a great delicacy and is more commonly found in deep water.*

sheltered bay behind this rocky reef is predominantly flat with a sand and shingle bottom interspaced with low rocky ridges that run parallel to the shore. The cliff face of the northern side of the bay is cut with numerous fissures where edible crabs (*Cancer pagarus*) can be found vying for territory with conger eels (*Conger conger*) and squat lobsters (*Galathea strigosa*).

The largest of the offshore reefs is known locally as Forley Craig and the near vertical walls make for some interesting dives due to the numerous fissures that are home to all manner of marine life including rockling, ling, and juvenile cod. Lobsters are always around, but it is much better to leave them there for the next person to admire the blue colour of the shell in the sea, rather than the orange colour of the shell on your plate in the local restaurant. It is essential to carry a torch at all times to explore the many crevices. There are octopus, tiny cuttlefish, and numerous shrimps that inhabit the area.

Most of the Catterline shore dives are not tide dependent, but care should be taken if you venture outside the bay, because you may encounter some current, which always runs parallel to the shore. Visibility is variable during the season and is entirely dependent on the wind. It can be quite poor around 10 ft (3 m), but during a long spell of offshore wind in late summer, the underwater visibility is excellent.

Scotland's submarine cliffs are a photographer's playground because they are usually crowded with marine life.

A diver takes a closer look at the common or edible sea urchin (Echinus esculentus). These urchins are algae eaters and can soon strip any rocks bare of encrusting seaweeds. ▶

Expertise Required:	1
Overall Grade:	1–2
Location:	Off the headland at Portsoy, Moray Firth
Typical Depth Range:	10–36 ft (3–12 m)
Typical Current Conditions:	Slight to moderate with surge to be expected
Access:	Directly from the shore

This is a nice easy dive for those visiting the Moray Firth shoreline. It is better along the eastern end due to the more rocky substrate. As you approach Inverness to the west, the rocky seabed is replaced by sand and then mud. The whole of the Moray Firth is well documented for the wreckage number—ships and material including tanks—caused by Heinkel bombers, during World War II.

The pleasant, interesting gullies and rock fissures yield the normal rocky kelp species to be expected, plus lobster, edible crabs, large numbers of sea urchins, octopi, and cuttlefish. The gulleys soon giveway to sand and there are always flounder and swimming crabs. A perfect dive for training.

The Moray Firth is also home to two large pods of Atlantic dolphins. Regular boat trips from the marina at Inverness will take you out into the bay where the dolphins will generally perform—as if trained. If you have the time, try the boat trip. Unfortunately, you are not allowed to swim with them.

4

Diving in Scapa Flow

Scapa Flow undoubtedly offers the best wreck diving in the British Isles and certainly ranks in the top five wreck-diving areas of the world. There are more shipwrecks in Scapa Flow than any other location on the planet. This deep, formidable, cold, natural harbour has served the warring nations' fleets for centuries. Considered by many to be impregnable to attack, the bay covers some 120 mi^2 (190 km^2) and is completely sheltered by a ring of protective islands. Situated 15 mi (25 km) north of the Scottish mainland, access is by the daily car ferry from Scrabster or by regular flight to Kirkwall airport from Edinburgh and Aberdeen.

A brief look at Scapa Flow's history explains the abundance of wrecks. Taking advantage of the internment to save the the Imperial Fleet from further disgrace and not having been informed properly over the reasons for the Armistice being surrendered on 21 June 1919, Admiral Ludwig

The Dresden is another of the light cruisers that were deliberately sunk on orders of Admiral Von Reuter in 1919.

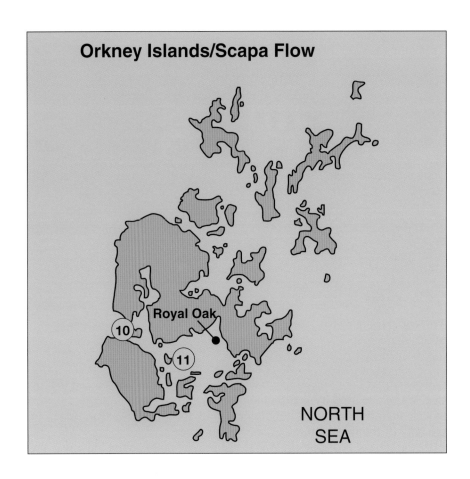

Orkney Islands/Scapa Flow

NORTH
SEA

Scapa Flow Dive Sites	Skill Level			Site Rating			
	Beginner	Intermediate	Advanced	1	2	3	4
H.M.S *Royal Oak*	(not open to the public)						
10 *Inverlane*		x	x		x	x	x
11 *Brummer*			x				x

Dive site ratings:

1—Easy shore dive and snorkelling, little current
2—Shallow reef dive from shore or boat, little to mild current
3—Deeper dive to offshore reef or wall, always current
4—Deep dive to wreck or reef, and/or strong current

The Scapa Flow dive boat Jean Elaine *pulls in to the pier at the old naval base at Lyness on the island of Hay in the Orkney Islands.*

von Reuter was convinced that war conditions were reinstated and that his fleet was to be used by their enemies against their homeland. He decided to save their honour, so he deliberately sunk the fleet. This fleet makes up the bulk of the wrecks more accessible to divers.

At the start of hostilities in WWII, the protection of Scapa Flow was further reinforced by the use of 'block ships'. These were ships sunk deliberately to stop access into the bay by enemy shipping. At present there are 3 battleships, 4 light cruisers, 5 torpedo boats (destroyers), a WWII destroyer (F2), 2 submarines, 27 large sections of remains and salvors equipment, 16 known British wrecks, 32 blockships, and 2 battleships (the *Vanguard* and the *Royal Oak*), with a further 54 as yet unidentified.

Several boat charter operators now know these wrecks intimately and are able to provide all of the services you require. Much of the diving is in depths greater than 100 ft (30 m) and one of the operators now offers 'technical diving' with mixed gas systems. Conditions vary tremendously during the season and it is generally poor visibility and dark on the seabed, lights should always be used and work-up dives should be undertaken before you do the deeper battleships.

In between dives, the dive boats often anchor on the jetty at Lyness, the former naval base on the Island of Hoy. There is a museum nearby with an excellent display of artifacts relating to the two World Wars. The museums in both Stromness and Kirkwall are also well worth a visit. Kirkwall Cathedral has a special commemoration of H.M.S. *Royal Oak*.

H.M.S *Royal Oak*

On the night of October 14th 1939, the 600-foot (188 m) battleship *Royal Oak* was at anchor in the sheltered bay of Scapa Flow in the Orkney Islands. Her duties were to protect Kirkwall and the British fleet from aerial attack. With the outbreak of the Second World War the Orkney Islands and Scapa Flow remained the key to the Royal Navy's North Atlantic strategy. Scapa Flow was considered impenetrable because of the narrow passages between the reefs and islands. It was thought that an attack would be only from the skies, not from below.

Commander Gunther Prien of *U-47* led one of the most incredibly bold attacks ever recorded. Under cover of darkness and a fast incoming tide through Kirk Sound (now blocked permanently), his U-boat entered Scapa Flow, fired two salvos of torpedos at the *Royal Oak* and escaped to open water as the *Royal Oak* and 833 men perished in these cold north Atlantic waters. Kirk Sound was both narrow and shallow and was further hampered by block ships. No one would have dreamt that Commander Gunther Prien could have dared such a hazardous route, or imagined his success.

Prien's first salvo of two torpedos at 1 o'clock in the morning inflicted only minor damage and confused the crew of the *Royal Oak* into thinking the muffled explosions were an on-board problem. This gave Commander

This is the steam pinnace that was pulled under and sunk when H.M.S. Royal Oak *was sunk by the German U-47 on 14 October 1939.*

The Ensign flag flies once more, now underwater attached to the starboard propeller shaft of H.M.S. Royal Oak *in honor of the lives lost on her.*

Prien an additional 20 minutes in which to reload and fire a second salvo, which gave three direct hits and sent the *Royal Oak* to the seabed in less than ten minutes.

She now rests upside down in 100 ft (33 m) of water, her decks at 45°. Her keel, camouflaged by more than 55 years of marine growth is now encrusted in kelp, soft corals, and anemones. It has the appearance of an underwater cliff and, as you descend, more and more of the superstructure is covered in anemones, tube worms, brittlestarfish and many varieties of fish, shrimps, and crabs.

The hull comes to within 15 ft (5 m) of the surface, and it is here that the Royal Navy Clearance Diving Team make their annual pilgrimage to ceremoniously unfold the battle ensign and once more fly this flag from the stern of the *Royal Oak* in the memory of the 833 officers and men who lost their lives. The battle ensign is attached to the starboard propellor shaft, which now rests at a depth of 50 ft (15 m). The exact location is marked by a large green channel buoy, although this is not necessary due to the fuel oil that still leaks out to the surface and serves as a poignant reminder to the dramatic events that happened on the night of October 14, 1939.

The Royal Oak is now a designated war grave and is protected by Navy Law. Diving on her is strictly forbidden, and it is only on the anniversary of her sinking that a team of elite Navy divers is allowed to descend through these chilly waters that conceal her watery grave. As the only

The Churchill Barriers were built in the Orkney islands to block all entry into the eastern approaches of Scapa Flow as a result of the sinking of H.M.S. Royal Oak.

civilian allowed to accompany the Royal Navy and record the flag ceremony on film, I felt it a great honour and privilege to dive H.M.S. *Royal Oak.* A book on the history of her sinking is due for publication soon.

As a direct result of the sinking of H.M.S. *Royal Oak,* the eastern approaches to Scapa Flow were completely blocked by the now-famous Churchill Barriers.

Stromness harbour in the Orkney Islands has remained virtually unchanged over the centuries when it used to be a whaling village, now home to most of the dive charter boats which are used in Scapa Flow.

Expertise Required:	2
Overall Grade:	2–4
Location:	Burra Sound entrance to Scapa Flow, Orkney Islands
Typical Depth Range:	10–30 ft (3–8 m)
Typical Current Conditions:	Wreck sits in a tidal race, so care must always be taken; an experienced boat handler is essential (with local knowledge)
Access:	By boat only

Although situated at the entrance of Burra Sound in Scapa Flow, the dive itself is actually inside the wreck (actually only half of the wreck, the remains of the stern are near Whitburn off the Northumberland coast). You do not venture outside of the wreck as there is a good chance of being swept off, making it very difficult to locate you later. The *Inverlane* is one of many block ships sunk during the Second World War to deter enemy ships from entering Scapa Flow, which was the naval base of the Home Fleet.

The bows are completely clear of the water and the dive boat that you are on will tie up alongside the stricken vessel. The dive plan is to climb

The rear section of the blockship Inverlane *is blasted open, but divers are advised to go no farther because of the dangerous currents.*

A diver exits from the blockship Inverlane *at Burra Sound, at the western entrance to Scapa Flow.*

onto the wreck with all of your kit, assemble and dive in through one of the many hatches into the hold. The water is always clear inside and the deteriorating ribs and spars are covered in the dwarf species of plumose anemones, which come in three colour variations. Cushion starfish can also be found on the superstructure. Small schools of sand eels take shelter in the largest of the holds and jellyfish seem to pulsate as they glide past you, trailing their stinging tentacles behind.

Towards the bow, a more-than-friendly seal usually scares everyone when they first encounter it in the gloom. Towards the stern, the whole of the back end is blown away revealing a huge expanse of twisted metal some 30 feet square (9 m). You are able to sit and watch the current and schools of fish rush by. Slack water is only around ten minutes at the entrance to Burra sound, which is why it is recommended to stay inside the wreckage at all times.

Shafts of light play through the open hatchways, and there are several exits, depending on the state of the tide. It is a rather strange feeling to climb inside a ship wearing all of your diving gear and not to venture outside at all. An excellent dive and not to be missed, photographically it is much better than any of the 1919 German Fleet.

Expertise Required:	3
Overall Grade:	4
Location:	Scapa Flow, Orkney Islands
Typical Depth Range:	80–120 ft (25–36 m)
Typical Current Conditions:	Nil to slight
Access:	By boat only, generally from Stromness

The *Brummer* is one of the most photogenic light cruisers from what is left of the German High Seas Battle Fleet scuttled by Admiral Ludwig von Reuter in 1919. Designed and built in 1913, the *Brummer* was used effectively by laying mines in the paths of allied shipping. She was fast enough (34 knots) to outrun any vessel that could overpower her by gunfire, and also had enough firepower of her own to engage the enemy. Joining the High Seas Fleet in 1916, she carried 360 mines and four 5.9-inch guns (150mm), displaced 4,000 tons and was 460 feet long (140 m).

She finally sank on Saturday, 21 June 1919, and now rests on her starboard side in 123 ft of water (37 m). With a sharp bow silhoutte that sweeps to the left she is very recognisable. Rapidly deteriorating, it is now advised not to enter the ship, due to the rapid drop in visibility from rust particles and sedimentation. The main superstructure is still intact and the

The kelp-fringed bow of the Brummer, *scuttled in Scapa Flow in 1919, now lies at 120 ft (37 m).*

guns are still in position, pointing astern. Large holes are now around the bridge and main companionway. At the stern, the rudder is now on the seabed and the propeller and shaft are long gone, being easily accessible, they were always the first parts of the ships to be salvaged.

The superstructure is covered in brittle starfish, sea squirts, feather stars (*Antedon bifida*), sea urchins, and crabs. Large plumose anemones have attached themselves onto the outer railings and guns and the seabed is littered with shell debris. The *Brummer* is a fascinating wreck and one of the best in Scapa Flow, certainly much better than the massive battleships *Kronprinz Wilhelm, Markgraf,* and the *Konig.* Other notable wrecks are the *Dresden, Koln,* and the *Karlsruhe.* The WW2 destroyer *F2* is also interesting and shallow at only 55 ft (17 m).

A diver swims along the hull of the Brummer, *one of the German High Seas Battle Fleet scuttled in Scapa Flow in 1919.*

5

Diving in the Shetland Islands

The Shetland Islands, Britain's most northerly archipelago, comprise more than 100 islands, of which 20 are inhabited. Lying 50 miles northeast of the Orkney Islands, the capital of the Shetlands, Lerwick, is actually farther north than the southernmost tip of Greenland!

Off the north and west, exceptional clear water is the norm and the walls and canyons are covered in a profusion of marine life. Diving is done by boat, conditions are variable and generally very windy, however, during the summer months the Islands are beautiful, and always historically interesting. You can take the ferry from Aberdeen, Kirkwall, or Norway, or fly into Sumburgh Airport on the mainland. Several of the smaller islands are also connected by car ferry and small aircraft. There are a couple of car hire companies located at the airport.

Passing through one of the many fascinating canyons in the Shetland Islands.

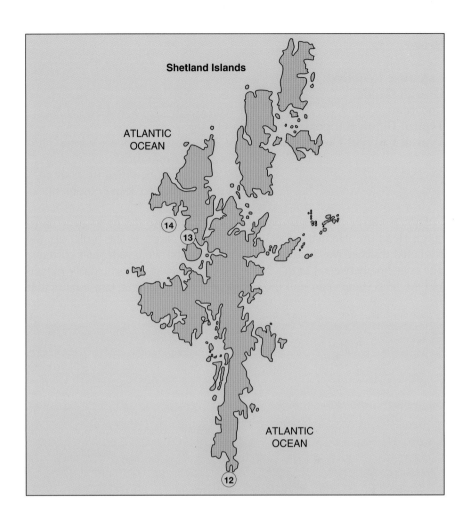

Shetland Islands Dive Sites	Skill Level			Site Rating			
	Beginner	Intermediate	Advanced	1	2	3	4
12 *Braer*		x	x		x	x	
13 Brei Ness, Muckle Roe		x	x		x	x	
14 The Drongs, Hillswick		x	x			x	

Dive site ratings:

1—Easy shore dive and snorkelling, little current
2—Shallow reef dive from shore or boat, little to mild current
3—Deeper dive to offshore reef or wall, always current
4—Deep dive to wreck or reef, and/or strong current

49

Expertise Required:	2
Overall Grade:	2–3
Location:	Between Garth's Ness and Siggar Ness
Typical Depth Range:	50 ft (15 m)
Typical Current Conditions:	Slight, but subject to severe winter storms and oceanic surge
Access:	By boat only, can be dived from shore, but is a very long walk in equipment

The oil tanker *Braer* was abandoned to drift onto the rocks near Sumburgh Head on 5 January, 1993. Shedding her cargo as she broke up, the predicted disaster was fortunately avoided by the wind, tide, and currents. The coastline between Garth's Ness and Siggar Ness is particularly rugged and the tidal streams around the corner of Fitful Head can cause particular

The bow of the infamous shipwreck Braer *still juts out above the surface in the Shetland Islands.*

The common starfish (Asterias rubens) *is seen here moving amongst the small sea squirt* (Dendrodoa grossularia). *These starfish are found all around the British isles.*

concern when approaching the shipwreck, but generally the sea conditions around the *Braer* are suitable. The bow still stand clear of the water.

The underwater visibility can be 12–20 ft (4–6 m), which proved a hindrance in trying to identify sections of the ship, plus the fact that the ship is now completely broken up. The superstructure now consists of a series of flattened overlapping plates, and every available part of ferrous metal has been carpeted by the kelp plants (*Laminaria saccharina* and *Alaria esculenta*). The deck railings are also covered in this algae. The larger sections of metal around the stern and directly next to the shore are also covered in barnacles (*Balanus balanus*) and the common starfish (*Asterias rubens*).

The remains of the *Braer* are spread out over a vast area with very few parts coming close to the surface. One section near the stern is wedged against the rocks on the shore and the only other large section of the ship is the bow, which still stands clear some 9–12 ft (3–4 m). Again, this area of the wreck is covered in algae, except where the anti-fouling paint still has a grip, but even this is being overgrown by an algal 'fuzz'. Overall this is an interesting dive, particularly in light of her history.

Brei Ness, Muckle Roe 13

Expertise Required:	2
Overall Grade:	2–3
Location:	West coast of Muckle Roe
Typical Depth Range:	40–100 ft (12–30 m)
Typical Current Conditions:	Slight to moderate, with some surge
Access:	By boat only from Muckle Roe Marina

This gulley on the northern edge of Muckle Roe (Big Red) has three deep caves at the base of the cliff wall. The caves travel quite far into the cliff and always have schools of sand eels at the entrances, similar to the silversides one encounters in the Caribbean or even glassfish in the Red Sea. At the entrance of the bay, a fault of softer stone has eroded away and created a vertical canyon that runs parallel to the shore.

Muckle Roe Marina is the base for the dive boat from the Brae Hotel, operated by Joe Rocks.

A diver has encountered a large pelagic jellyfish (Rhizostoma pulmo) *common on the west coast during the summer months.*

As you travel north, into the main body of the canyon the depth starts at 12 m and gradually slopes down to more than 100 ft (30 m). The narrow sides are variable in distance apart and the sandy bottom is often covered in huge tumbled boulders more than 10 ft across (3 m). The walls are carpeted in jewel anemones and it is here that the largest aggregation of large dahlia anemones (*Urticina felina*) can be found; there are thousands of these brightly coloured anemones everywhere you look. Interspaced along the walls you can also find sea squirts, squat lobsters, spider crabs, and edible crabs. Large, pelagic lions' mane jellyfish move slowly through the canyon with a host of juvenile herring that flit amongst the stinging tentacles, seemingly immune to the stinging cells. These gulleys are some of the most picturesque I have dived.

The Drongs, Hillswick   14

Expertise Required: 2
Overall Grade: 3
Location: Offshore at Hillswick
Typical Depth Range: 10–50 ft (3–15 m)
Typical Current Conditions: Slight, but subject to surge being so far
                                   offshore
Access: By boat only

These rocky fangs are instantly recognisable and from a distance resemble the masts, rigging, and sails of an ancient sailing ship. Approachable only by boat, the journey time from Muckle Roe marina will take about 45 minutes.

The depth around the Drongs drops rapidly to 45 ft (15 m) and due to their particularly exposed location, there is a strong surge through the gul-

The Drongs, a series of vertical sea stacks, offer superb diving in the Shetlands.

leys. Very few divers ever get the chance to dive this site, but if the oppor-
tunity arises, please make the effort.

The uppermost portion of the rocks is covered in kelp and there are huge
boulders everywhere tumbling to the seabed 50 ft below (15 m). There is
much encrusting life including nudibranchs, small sponges, molluscs, and
crustaceans. Large colourful anemones can be found along the inner walls
as well as squat lobsters, common lobsters, and crayfish. The surge can be
a problem and care must be taken in not getting too close to the inner
canyons, where you can be pushed through to the other side, which makes
for a long swim back around to the dive boat's safe anchorage.

*This underhanging cliff is festooned with marine life and is a constant source of
wonder to the perceptive diver.*

6

Diving in the Outer Hebrides and Northwest Coast

Of all the Outer Hebridean Islands, Flannan Isles and the St. Kilda Archipelago are perhaps the most sought after by divers who want the ultimate in British waters diving. These offshore islands are rarely visited and then only during the summer months. The islands of Lewis, Harris, Benbecula, North and South Uist, Eriskay, Vatersay, Sandray, and Mingulay all yield superb diving. There are still many undived shipwrecks cited on the admiralty charts, and your dive boat will be accompanied by schools of pilot whales and porpoises whenever you pass through the channels between the islands.

The farther out into the Atlantic you travel, the clearer the water becomes, but it is also prone to sudden weather changes. An essential part of a good dive boat's equipment is a weather fax to keep abreast of any sudden changes. On one trip, we were weather-bound in an obscure sea loch on the west coast of the Isle of Lewis, unable to travel any farther because of the hurricane force winds; so we had some superb dives in what otherwise would have been an 'unexplored' area. There were pelicans' foot starfish, sea cucumbers, scallops, and the mussels were a culinary delight!

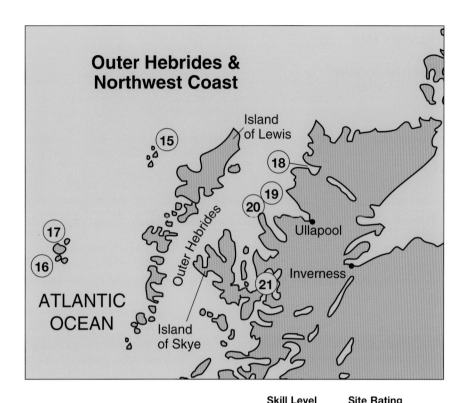

Outer Hebrides & Northwest Coast

Island of Lewis

ATLANTIC OCEAN

Ullapool

Inverness

Outer Hebrides

Island of Skye

Outer Hebrides and Northwest Coast Dive Sites	Skill Level			Site Rating			
	Beginner	Intermediate	Advanced	1	2	3	4
15 Flannan Isle		x	x		x	x	
16 the Sawcut, St. Kilda		x	x		x	x	
17 Sgarbstac, Boreray, St. Kilda			x				x
18 South Ferry Slip, Kylesku Narrows			x			x	x
19 Horse Island		x	x			x	x
20 Conservation Cave, Tanera Beg		x	x			x	
21 *Port Napier*		x	x			x	x

Dive site ratings:

1—Easy shore dive and snorkelling, little current
2—Shallow reef dive from shore or boat, little to mild current
3—Deeper dive to offshore reef or wall, always current
4—Deep dive to wreck or reef, and/or strong current

◀ *Flannan Isle near the Outer Hebridean island of Lewis is home to some of the best diving in Scotland.*

Expertise Required:	2
Overall Grade:	2–3
Location:	22 mi (38km) northwest of the Isle of Lewis
Typical Depth Range:	10–50 ft (3–15 m)
Typical Current Conditions:	Slight to moderate with oceanic surge
Access:	By boat only

Sometimes referred to as the Seven Hunters, the seven islands that make up the Flannans are all exposed to the might of the Atlantic swell and landfalls are often difficult. They were described by Dr. J. MacCulloch in his *Description of the Western Isles* in 1824, 'like a meadow thickly enamelled with daisies'. All of the Flannans are rich in bird life and during the months of May and June you will be accompanied underwater by shags and kittiewakes.

The softer rock substrate has been eroded away over the centuries to make some spectacular caves and natural archways. Diving is possible through most of them, but a few are subject to strong currents and surge, which makes for exhilarating diving to say the least. The walls are thickly carpeted in jewel anemones, small sea quirts, and brittle starfish. Cuckoo wrasse (*Labrus mixtus*) are curious and approach your camera lens a little too closely, and lesser-spotted dogfish are common (*Scyliorhinus canicula*). The common seal can also be found around the entrances to the caves where there is a rich forest of kelp. Although difficult to reach, the Flannan Isles are superb diving and every effort should be made to travel out into the Atlantic.

The cuckoo wrasse swim in small mating groups; the females are a drab brown compared to the more brightly coloured males.

Expertise Required:	2
Overall Grade:	2–3
Location:	Island of Dun, Village Bay, St. Kilda
Typical Depth Range:	10–60 ft (3–18 m)
Typical Current Conditions:	Moderate, with surge conditions occasionally
Access:	By boat only

Thirty-four miles (54 km) WNW of North Uist in the Outer Hebrides, the St. Kilda Archipelago is the most westerly inhabited island in Europe, and then only by the military and seasonal wardens for the National Trust for Scotland. These extremely remote islands were originally inhabited by a native population that was finally evacuated in 1930 due to deprivation and disease. The islands are also so effectively cut off from all civilisation, there are even indigenous species of animals that are found nowhere else in the British Isles. The St. Kilda Wren, St. Kilda Mouse, and Soay Sheep have evolved over the centuries on these remote islands. The ruins of many of the former buildings on the main island of Hirta can still be seen today and a number are now being renovated by volunteers with the National Trust for Scotland.

Plaice (Pleuronectes platessa) seen here on a sandy seabed has reddish spots along its back and is much sought after for the commercial fishing markets.

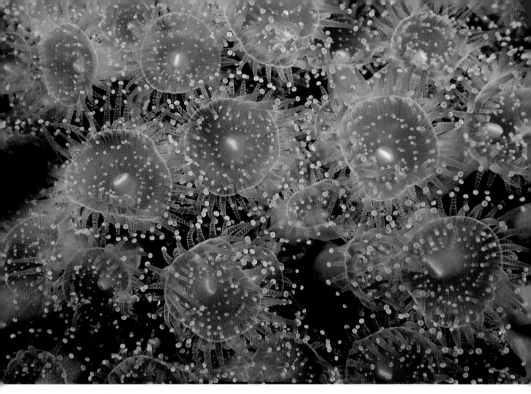

The jewel anemone (Corynactis viridis) *is more commonly found around the outer islands on the west and north coast of Scotland.*

The Sawcut is a vertical slice into the Island of Dun, which is a national bird sanctuary. The kelp forest in these offshore islands reaches depths of 80 ft (25 m) and fringes the sides of the canyon. With the reduction of light, the kelp forest stops and the walls are covered in soft corals, anemones, sea squirts, and starfish. Small schools of fish hover around and seals often venture in to see what the divers are up to.

Underneath the mooring in Village Bay is also interesting at night, with many octopus, shrimp, and hermit crabs. Village Bay is completely sheltered from the worst of the Atlantic storms and offers safe anchorage for your liveaboard dive boat.

Dive charter boat is the only way out to the islands as the aerial trips made by Bristows helicopters are reserved for emergency use, mail, and British Army personnel. The main island of Hirta is well worth exploring on foot and you should make the effort to climb to the top; the views are quite spectacular. The vertical cliffs here are the highest in the British Isles and the noise from the nesting seabirds in the spring is almost deafening. It is true to say that the hardest-to-reach diving locations also yield the highest potential for dives of above average quality.

Expertise Required:	3
Overall Grade:	4
Location:	To the southeast of Boreray, St. Kilda Archipelago
Typical Depth Range:	80–150 ft (25–45 m)
Typical Current Conditions:	Variable, but more subject to oceanic surge
Access:	By boat only

The St. Kilda group yields such a high proportion of superb dives that it would take a separate guide to do the islands justice. Bear in mind that it is only during the summer months that the charter dive boats are able to make the journey from Oban to these far-flung islands. If the weather does turn against you, the nearest safe shelter is Tarbert on the isle of Lewis. This seemingly ineffectual small rocky stac, or rock, is cut through by a huge underwater archway that starts at 100 ft (30 m). The archway is around 65 ft wide (20 m) and it is more than 100 ft (30 m) before you reach the other side. The walls and underhanging edge of this massive cavern are totally covered in all manner of life.

The walls drop well below the safe air diving depth and because of the clarity of the water, you must be extremely careful with your time and not exceed safe depth limits. Crabs, lobster, crayfish, sea urchins, and nudibranchs are everywhere amidst small encrusting sponges and fields of jewel anemones of every colour known to man. Incredibly picturesque and colourful, this dive will remain in your memories for years to come. This is regarded as diving at the edge of the world, and it is only when you realise how small and vulnerable you are in this huge ocean that the scale of the location hits home. It is a dive not to be undertaken lightly.

*This hermit crab's shell is overgrown with a fine hydroid 'fuzz', and the nudibranch (*Limacea clavigera*) has attached itself onto the crab's home to eat a hydroid.*

Expertise Required:	3
Overall Grade:	3–4
Location:	North of Lochinver to Kylesku and next to the old ferry slipway
Typical Depth Range:	10–100 ft (3–30 m)
Typical Current Conditions:	Fierce, over than 5 knots, so timing is critical to try and catch the slack water
Access:	Directly from the old ferry slipway and all around the area. It is often better to use an inflatable boat as back up, just in case divers are swept away

The problem as always with this type of site is the current. The best time is 45 minutes before low tide, when the tidal race is least. This will allow for a gentle drift dive along the wall travelling westwards. The cliff continues all the way down to 100 ft (30 m) and on around the next headland.

The walls of the cliff are covered in orange and white coft corals, huge dahlia anemones (*Urticina eques*), numerous sponges and the rare Devonshire cup coral (*Caryophyllia smithii*). With such a swift moving current

*The dahlia anemone (*Urticina felina*) comes in many colour variations and can often be found covering vast areas of rocky substrate.*

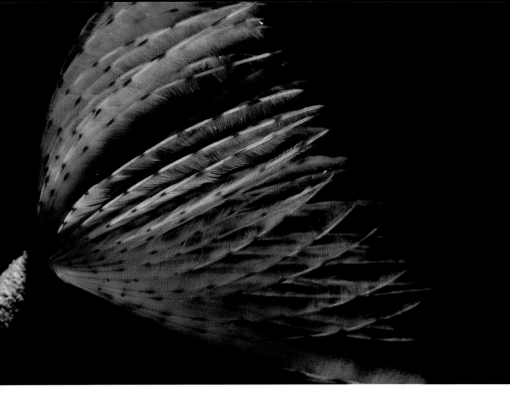

*Peacock worms (*Sabella penicillus*) are a regular feature of the west coast sea lochs; they are also found in much deeper water off the Scottish east coast.*

you would expect to find filter feeders of various varieties and the Peacock worm (*Sabella penicillus*) is very much in evidence. Lots of species of seaweeds are found in the shallows where small squat lobsters, sticklebacks, and suckerfish abound.

At 100 ft (30 m) on the seabed, large edible crabs can be found burrowing in the mud amidst large scallop shells. The rare pelican's foot starfish is also found here as well as the scampi prawn—sometimes referred to as the Norway lobster (*Nephrops norvegicus*). Pipefish are occasionally seen and there are always schools of fish along the walls.

There is very good car parking and toilets available.

*Turbot (*Scopthalmus maximus*) are larger members of the flounder or flatfish family, but more circular. They are grown commercially on many fish farms.*

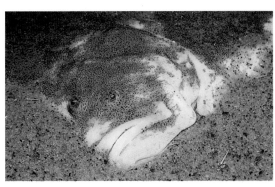

Expertise Required:	2
Overall Grade:	3–4
Location:	Deep dive offshore. Summer Isles
Typical Depth Range:	10–100 ft (3–30 m)
Typical Current Conditions:	Slight, but subject to oceanic swell
Access:	By boat only

The dive boat pick up is at Badentarbert Pier at Achiltibuie, northwest of Ullapool. Atlantic Diving Services operates from the large island opposite the pier called Tanera Mhor. The 20 minutes it takes to reach the dive site on board the M.V. *Heron,* is best spent getting kitted up and ready to enter the water when you arrive. There is no anchor drop and the boat's skipper will drift around this small island and pick you up after your allowed time, depending on the depth you plan. Here you have a vertical wall that drops to 50 ft (15 m), followed by a steep sandy slope to beyond 100 ft (30 m).

The uppermost part of the cliff is covered in sugar kelp, which is always untidy looking, but once below this, you'll find the cliff covered in sea squirts, brittle starfish, and feather starfish. Underneath the rocky ledges can be found the long-clawed squat lobster (*Munida rugosa*). Farther down you can find sea pens, horse mussels, and scallops. Nudibranchs can be found on some of the sponges and soft corals. Dahlia anemones and plumose anemones are also common.

The M.V. Heron *is the dive boat operated by Atlantic Diving Services in the Summer Isles west of Ullapool.*

Expertise Required:	2
Overall Grade:	3
Location:	On the outer edge and south of the Summer Isles, west of Ullapool
Typical Depth Range:	10–100 ft (3–30 m)
Typical Current Conditions:	Slight, but subject to oceanic swell
Access:	By boat only

This has got to be one of the best dives in the Summer Isles; however, it is often difficult due to the oceanic swell that pounds into the cave. This is an attractive site above and below the water. At the far end of the shallow cave there is a hole in the roof that casts a shaft of light down into the depths. Approaching underwater from the seaward side, your passage is

Black brittle starfish (Ophiocomina nigra) inhabit much of the deeper areas of seabed below 100 ft (30 m).

Sun starfish (Crossaster papposus) prey upon the brittle starfish.

almost blocked by some huge, rounded boulders that are fairly well stripped of life except for low encrusting sponges, sea squirts, and soft corals.

The wall to the south extends from the cave and drops down rapidly to well over 100 ft (30 m). It is absolutely covered in jewel anemones (*Corynactis viridis*) and many species of nudibranchs. Brittle starfish become more profuse as the dive deepens away from the cave and soon all of the rocky surfaces are covered by this wriggling mass of spiky arms. Here they are preyed upon by the sun starfish (*Crossaster papposus*). This truly is a very colourful dive, visibility is always good, there is little current to speak of, and the only real danger is being swept into the rocks by the surge. The Marine Conservation Society named this cave during one of their many expeditions to this superb area of bays, inlets, and islands.

Expertise Required:	2
Overall Grade:	3–4
Location:	Kyle of Lochalsh, Island of Skye
Typical Depth Range:	Surface–66 ft (0–20 m)
Typical Current Conditions:	To be expected, moderate to strong
Access:	By boat only

A minelayer of 9,600 tons, the *Port Napier* was lost by fire in 1940 just 1,000 ft (300 m) from the Skye shoreline, near the Kyle of Lochalsh. At over 500 ft long (150 m), the Port Napier is a very popular dive. However, not all of the cargo has been cleared and there are still mines and ammunition on board, so care should always be taken when probing the interior. The wreck is quite easy to find as she lies on her side in only 66 ft (20 m) of water on a muddy bottom. A vertical spar projects above the surface of the water and part of the hull is visible at low tide. Boats are usually launched from Kyle of Lochalsh or Kyleakin.

As an underwater photographer, I rate this wreck quite high on my list as there is always lots to photograph; although not primarily interested in scrap metal, I am more interested in the profuse, colonising marine life. Leaving the Kyle of Lochalsh, you will pass by Eilean Donan Castle, which is very distinctive and has featured in many films including *Highlander*.

The elegant anemone (Sagartia elegans) grows to only 1 in. across (3cm) and is found in large aggregations of various colour forms.

7

Diving in the Inner Hebrides and West Coast

The Inner Hebrides and Small Isles are situated between the Scottish mainland and the Outer Hebrides. The Small Isles are Canna (with Sanday), Rum, Eigg, and Muck. To the northeast is Skye. To the south lie Coll, Tiree, Colonsay, Mull, Iona, Jura, and Islay, names which conjure up the particular tastes of malt whiskies distilled on the islands. Being protected from the worst of the Atlantic storms, these islands are a favourite with visiting divers, and because very little underwater exploration has taken place, there are still many exciting finds to make and undived wrecks marked enticingly on the Admiralty charts.

Divers approaching the dive boat after another exploration underwater.

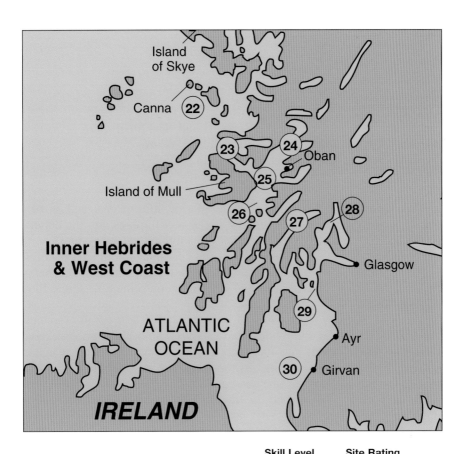

Island of Skye

Canna (22)

Island of Mull

(23)

(24) Oban

(25)

Inner Hebrides & West Coast

(26)

(27)

(28)

Glasgow

ATLANTIC
OCEAN

(29)

Ayr

(30) Girvan

IRELAND

Inner Hebrides and West Coast Dive Sites	Skill Level			Site Rating			
	Beginner	Intermediate	Advanced	1	2	3	4
22 Sgeir a'Phuirt, Canna	x	x	x			x	x
23 *Hispania*			x			x	x
24 Falls of Lora			x			x	x
25 Heather Island, Oban		x	x			x	x
26 Insh Island, Oban		x	x			x	x
27 Kenmore Point	x	x	x		x	x	x
28 The Submarine Pens, Loch Long		x	x			x	x
29 Catalina, Isle of Combrae, Firth		x	x		x	x	
30 Ailsa Craig		x	x		x	x	

Dive site ratings:

1—Easy shore dive and snorkelling, little current
2—Shallow reef dive from shore or boat, little to mild current
3—Deeper dive to offshore reef or wall, always current
4—Deep dive to wreck or reef, and/or strong current

Expertise Required:	1
Overall Grade:	3–4
Location:	Canna Island, The Small Isles
Typical Depth Range:	10–120 ft (3–37 m)
Typical Current Conditions:	Very little
Access:	By boat only

This dive site is extremely rich in marine life species and is best approached from the north. This low, rocky reef tumbles into the depths; the steep, near vertical wall is actually a jumbled series of rocks with many hiding places for squat lobsters, sea cucumbers, and small scorpionfish, shrimps, and prawns. In the shallower areas between the rocky reef and the island, seals abound and you can spend some time snorkelling amongst them.

The wall drops to 85 ft (26 m) and is covered in soft corals, sponges, and sea squirts. Near the boulder base, large plumose anemones extend their fine tentacles out into the slight current to trap nutrients. Cuckoo wrasse, ballan wrasse, saithe, and pollack are also evident. As you descend to the seabed, the fine sand and muddy bottom slopes off to the north and east. The seabed is literally crammed full of burrowing anemones (*Cerianthus lloydi*) as well as the burrowing starfish (*Astropecten*). This is an excellent dive site and on everyone's list as they explore these inner isles.

*The angel shark (*squatina squatina*) is a rare visitor to our shores and is a rather docile animal lying in wait on the sand for its prey to swim by.*

Expertise Required:	3
Overall Grade:	3–4
Location:	Sound of Mull, near Oban
Typical Depth Range:	50–100 ft (15–30 m)
Typical Current Conditions:	Must be dived at slack water as current can reach up to 3 knots
Access:	By boat only

The wreck is easily found by diving 60 ft (18 m) down the bouy that usually marks her location. Occasionally this gets lost, but there is another nearby where you can align yourself. Considered by some to be one of the best wrecks in Scottish waters outside Scapa Flow, I find it difficult due to the strong currents sometimes encountered. At 263 ft long (81 m), this small steamer weighed 1,340 tons and sunk in 1956 carrying a cargo of asbestos mats.

Over the years the boat has deteriorated, but safe access is still available in several areas. Care must be taken when entering the wreck and only those qualified should do so. Due to the frequent currents that pass through the sound of Mull, the wreck is literally blanketed in plumose anemones (*Metridium senile*), with virtually every bit of available space taken up. Schools of pollack, saithe, and cod are always about, and numerous spider crabs inhabit some of the darker holes. Conger eels are also found in the vicinity.

An experienced boat handler with knowledge of the tidal streams is essential; because of the current, timing is critical, but this is an exciting dive and thoroughly recommended. The wreck of the *Rondo* lies to the south of the Sound of Mull and these two wrecks should not be missed. Access is from the several dive centres that are found in the Sound of Mull as well as the dive charter boats that operate out of Oban.

One of the most common jellyfishes in the world, Aurelia aurita *is commonly associated with juvenile fish that seek protection from predators within the jellyfish's stinging tentacles.*

Expertise Required:	3
Overall Grade:	3–4
Location:	At the entrance to Loch Etive, Connel Bridge, near Oban
Typical Depth Range:	20–60 ft (6–18 m)
Typical Current Conditions:	Can reach up to 6 knots, so slack water is recommended
Access:	From the north or south shores directly under the bridge, but boat cover is essential

There are exhilarating drift dives and then there are the Falls of Lora. This site has no slack water; the current just seems to change direction. On the surface it may be flowing out of Loch Etive, yet when you approach the bottom, you find that you are being swept along into the loch and the deeper pools. This plays havoc if you are using a surface marker bouy, which is why boat cover is essential.

There are gullies and canyons that have been carved out of the rock, and the walls are covered in mussels, sponges, small scorpionfish, green crabs, and forests of dahlia anemones of every hue and colour. On the inside of one of the skerries, which is clear of the surface at low tide, there is quite a drop and shelter can be found from the current, but as it increases, you MUST NOT linger. Clearer water is always found as the tide rises and pushes into the loch. During the winter months the rainwater run-off from the hills reduces the visibility drastically and can make the dive even more dangerous than it should be.

Here a diver has stopped to examine some marine life next to a huge boulder topped with kelp.

Expertise Required:	2
Overall Grade:	3—4
Location:	South of Oban
Typical Depth Range:	10–100 ft (3–30 m).
Typical Current Conditions:	Slight to moderate.
Access:	By boat only

Heather Island is also a boat dive and access is from any number of slipways in the Oban harbour area. This small island lies off the east coast of the Island of Kerrera, the largest island on the way to Mull. To the north of the island is a shallow wall that drops to 35 ft (11 m) and the eastern wall drops rapidly to more than 100 ft (30 m). At the midway point along this eastern side there is also a sea cave, but only those with cave diving experience should venture into the chimney and beyond into the cavern as it has been the scene of a fatality in recent years.

The wall is covered in sea squirts (*Ciona intestinalis*) and the usual flora and fauna associated with the Scottish sea lochs, such as squat lobsters, many species of starfish and spider crabs, soft corals, and anemones. Here, you also can find the much rarer northern sea fan and peacock worms. Many other types of hydroids are found, and dogfish, a smaller species of shark, are also seen regularly. They lay their egg cases on the kelp stalks. There is current on this dive, but nothing too strong; however, this is a major boat lane and care should always be taken when using a smaller inflatable craft. This is a nice wall dive with many interesting forms of marine life, close to the launch sites of Oban.

*The bloody Henry starfish (*Henricia sanguinolenta*) is seen here crawling over an encrusting sponge on one of the submarine cliff walls.*

Insh Island, Oban 26

Expertise Required:	2
Overall Grade:	3–4
Location:	South of Oban, near Easedale
Typical Depth Range:	20–140 ft (6–43 m)
Typical Current Conditions:	Moderate to strong on the eastern approaches
Access:	By boat only, launching from Easedale across the slate beach near the old flooded quarry (which can also be dived if the sea is too rough)

Insh Island is long and narrow and is found to the northwest of Seil Island. This offshore dive has some very interesting species of sponge, soft and hard corals, and large numbers of sea squirts of various types. This very deep dive is fascinating, but be alert because much of the western wall is slightly overhanging and you can drop well below 140 ft (43 m) before you realise where you are. Great care should be taken with your dive profile.

The shallower reaches of the wall are covered in sugar kelp, which always looks untidy because it is always overgrown with hydroids, which attract sedimentation. The deeper you go along the wall, the clearer the water, but be careful of your bouyancy. The southern point is much more gently inclined and soon falls away in a jumbled series of huge boulders.

The deep-water dahlia anemone (Urticina eques) is distinguishable by the lack of sticky tubercles on its skin. These animals are found below 60 ft (18 m).

Kenmore Point   27

Expertise Required:	1
Overall Grade:	2–4
Location:	South of Inverary, Loch Fyne
Typical Depth Range:	10–100 ft (3–30 m)
Typical Current Conditions:	Slight
Access:	From shore, but boat cover can assist if required

This is one of the best dives in Loch Fyne, the second longest sea loch in Scotland at 41 miles long (66 km). Access is along a 3-mi (5-km) private road and forestry track, and the privacy signs should be obeyed. Entry is from either side of the small village. There is a rough gravel slipway to the north and a gravel beach to the south of the small headland with its vertical cliffs that drop to a mud slope at 80 ft (25 m). The slope

*Velvet swimming crabs (*Macropipus puber*) are very aggressive, and when approached will raise their pincers in defence and attack.*

shelves away rapidly and there are scallops, dragonets, large whelks, and edible crabs. When boat cover is required, or you wish to do the dive from the seaward side, then launching facilities are available from Inverary to the north and Strachur on the opposite shore.

The wall is the most interesting part of the dive, starting at 7 ft (2 m) it drops vertically and is cut by several narrow horizontal fissures. Here you can find the squat lobster (*Munida rugosa*) and the rare anemone (*Protanthia simplex*), which I first discovered here in 1975. Large brilliantly coloured dahlia anemones can also be found, as well as sea squirts, feather starfish, and brittle starfish. The slight current assists your swim around the corner to the exit.

Visibility is generally always good, except after prolonged and heavy rainfall. The fresh water run-off into the loch creates a layer of peat coloured water on the surface. Under this dark layer, the water is always clear, but the light has been blocked so drastically that lights must be used to illuminate the varied marine life on the wall and mud slope.

Farther south from Kenmore Point is Stallion Rock, which is similar in profile, but is in fact a single rock that rises from the muddy seabed 100 ft below (30 m). To the north of Kenmore, in Inverary, the old pier offers excellent night diving. Being only 26 ft deep (8 m), it is perfect for exploration and nudibranch hunting. Inverary Castle is home to the Duke and Duchess of Argyll.

*Squat lobster (*Munida rugosa*).*

Expertise Required:	2
Overall Grade:	3–4
Location:	Just north of the Royal Navy Base of Faslane on the shore of Loch Long, north of Glasgow
Typical Depth Range:	10–100 ft (3–30 m)
Typical Current Conditions:	Slight to moderate
Access:	Directly from the shore next to the car park

As you travel north along the eastern shores of Loch Long, there is a car park just beyond the Royal Naval Base at Faslane. There are few areas along this road where you can park and this is one of the most convenient for diving. There is a bit of a scramble over the rocky foreshore, but the seabed falls away rapidly down a steep muddy slope.

Visibility is variable, but generally clearer, the deeper you descend. The pleasure of diving on such a slope is that you are always on the seabed, and you can vary your dive profile exactly as it should be in the book, so the site is a favourite place for training. Coupled with many interesting forms of marine life such as sea pens, sea cucumbers, burrowing anemones, hermit crabs, gurnard, dogfish, and flounders, this makes for some interesting diving. Some of the rocky areas are encrusted with sea squirts, mussels, and squat lobsters. The kelp at the shoreline also has pipefish and numerous nudibranchs.

*This nudibranch (*Eubranchus farrani*) is but one of the fanciful creatures that add colour to just about any dive along Scotland's coast.*

Expertise Required:	2
Overall Grade:	2–3
Location:	300 ft (90 m) south of the ferry slipway on the Isle of Cumbrae, Firth of Clyde
Typical Depth Range:	66 ft (20 m).
Typical Current Conditions:	Slight to moderate occasionally
Access:	From the shore or by boat if required

A Catalina seaplane sank at its mooring just after WWII. Although still fairly intact, this is a popular site with many of the west coast dive clubs and it sometimes takes a battering from misplaced fins. Please take care when diving on this old seaplane. The wings are covered in plumose anemones (*Metridium senile*), sea squirts, and several different species of starfish including the large *Marthasterias glacialis.*

It is possible to enter the fusilage, but this is now home to an increasing number of conger eels, which, although not harmful, can give you a nasty fright when you least expect it. Visibility is variable along this stretch of the coastline due to the fresh water from the River Clyde and the surrounding islands. It is best dived during the summer months when there is less rain.

The seabed is a jumble of black brittle starfish and seemingly hundreds of hermit crabs (*Pagurus bernhardus*). Also on this muddy slope you may be fortunate to find the spiny starfish (*Astropecten*), which is generally buried in the sand.

Although generally considered aggressive, conger eels (Conger conger) are more inquisitive and will follow divers to see what they are up to.

Ailsa Craig   30

Expertise Required:	2
Overall Grade:	2–3
Location:	Volcanic sea stac, 10 miles west of Girvan (16 km)
Typical Depth Range:	10–120 ft (3–37 m)
Typical Current Conditions:	Variable, depending on location around the Island
Access:	By boat, generally from Girvan or Ayr

Often referred to as Paddy's Milestone, Ailsa Craig lies on the sea route between Scotland and Ireland when travelling from the Clyde ports. This massive granite rock rises 1,114 ft (304 m) and has a circumference of 2 miles (3 km). Incidentally, the granite from the island is used to make curling stones for the ancient, traditional Scottish game on ice.

Diving conditions are variable, depending on the time of year, and the underwater visibility is often notoriously bad. However, there are some very interesting dives around the precipitous cliffs of the rock. Swine Cave to the north falls vertically to 50 ft (15 m) then a steep muddy slope falls away into the depths. The wreck of the *Duke of Edinburgh* to the south lies in 120 ft of water (36 m). This former paddle steamer is now well broken up, but covered in all manner of marine life. The usual wrasse, pollack, and saithe are evident. Plumose anemones, squat lobsters, edible crabs, and hydroids are found on the sheer cliffs, and burrowing anemones and brittle starfish are found on the muddy slopes.

A diver passes over a large shoal of Atlantic salmon.

8

Overview of Scottish Marine Life

The Family Groups

Most types of marine life are relatively unknown to the average reader without specific knowledge of marine biology, so I will first give a summary of the groups of plants and animals to be found around the Scottish coast.

*Hydroid (*Tubularia indivisa*).*

Nurse hounds (Scyliorhinus stellaris) are a member of the shark family and are more common around the west coast islands.

Porifera or sponges, are animals of so simple a structure that they are more like an aggregation or colony of protozoans. They are always attached.

Coelenterata include a large number of relatively simple animals. There are two major groups: attached, like the anemones; and free swimming, like the jellyfish. Many of the attached are not solitary like the anemones, but consist of many united individuals like the hydroid *Tubularia indivisa.* Allied more closely to the anemones are the soft corals, or *Alcyonarians,* which consist of many individuals with a common skeleton of a horny substance and the true corals, *Scleractina,* with massive calcareous skeletons.

Turbellaria, or flat worms, are seldom more than 2.5 cm long, flat, transparent and sometimes parasitic.

Nemertina, soft-bodied worms, have a proboscis but lack the division of the body into transverse segments.

Tunicata are exclusively marine and comprise many animals of different appearance. This group includes the sea squirts and ascidians.

Annelida include the common lugworm, in which you can easily see the segments.

Polychate, bristleworms, are exclusively marine and include most marine worms. Many wander freely (errant worms) and others (sedentary worms) live in tubes of lime, sand or parchment-like material, which they make themselves and enlarge as they grow. Many of the types of worms have little in common with one another except their general shape.

Polyzoa are quite closely related to the bristleworms. These tiny creatures always live in colonies and have a horny skeleton. It is often found encrusting *Laminaria* species and seems to be the favourite diet of a number of sea slugs.

Echinodermata are a very diverse group, and include the starfish and sea urchin. They are mostly slow moving, locomotion being provided by the peculiar tube feet through a 'hydraulics' network of water supplied by canals throughout the body. There are five distinct groups : starfish, *Asteroidea;* brittlestars, *Ophiuroidea;* sea urchins, *Echinoidea;* sea cucumbers *Holothuroidea,* and finally feather stars and sea lillies, *Crinoidea.*

Arthropoda include the largest number of species of any group in the animal kingdom. Like annelid worms, they have segmented bodies, but have jointed limbs attached, which give the group its name.

Of the four great divisions, three—insect, spider, and centipede classes are almost exclusively found on land—and the fourth, *Crustacea,* is almost entirely marine. It is an all-embracing group that includes water fleas, barnacles, sand hoppers, shrimps, prawns, lobsters, hermit crabs, and many species of true crabs.

Mollusca form another group of considerable variety and include nudibranchs, chitons, and octopi. The *Gastropoda,* or univalved shellfish such as limpets, periwinkles, and snails, usually have a shell of one piece and live mostly on the shore or sea bottom, but a few with greatly reduced shells swim near the surface. *Bivalvia,* the bivalve molluscs, have a shell composed of more or less equal halves; another great division is the highly organised *Cephalopoda* which includes squid, octopi, and cuttlefish, distinguished by their eight or ten tentacles or arms. A similar group are the *Brachiapoda,* often mistaken for molluscs.

Fish are divided into two principal groups: *Elasmobranchs,* which include dogfish, sharks, and skate and have a relatively soft cartiliganous skeleton with separate gill openings; and *Teleosts,* or boney fish, which have hard boney skeletons and their gill openings are covered by flaps.

Scottish waters also are home to other animals more 'complex' than fish—'air breathers'. These creatures live on or near the surface and are capable of diving to considerable depths, though they are always compelled to return to the surface for air. *Cetacea* include whales, dolphins, and porpoises; and *Pinnepedea* include seals.

This group of sea urchins (Echinus esculentus) has stripped all the fronds from this kelp stalk. ▶

Appendix 1—Dive Centres and Services

Many of these facilities are PADI Five Star Facilities and all offer boat hire, instruction, equipment sales, etc. The list is included as a service to the reader and is as accurate as possible at the time of printing. This list does not constitute an endorsement of these facilities. If operators/owners wish to be included in future reprints/editions, please contact Pisces Books, P.O. Box 2608, Houston, Texas 77252-2608, USA.

Aberdeen Watersports
79 Waterloo Quay, Aberdeen.
Tel/Fax (44) 01224 581313

Aquatron
30 Stanley Street, Glasgow G42 1JB
Tel (44) 0141 429 5902
Fax (44) 0141 429 5364

Atlantic Diving Services
Port Cottage, Isle of Tanera Mhor
Achiltibuie,Ullapool IV26 2YN
Tel (44) 01854 622261
Fax (44) 01854 622401

Brae Hotel & Dive Charters
c/o Joe Rocks, Brae, Shetland Islands
Tel (44) 01806 522456
Fax (44) 01806 522459

C&C Marine Services
Largs Yacht Haven, Irvine Road
Largs, Ayrshire
Tel (44) 01475 687 180
Fax (44) 01475 687 388

Dive Shetland
c/o Alex Whitelaw, Bigton,
Shetland Islands
Tel (44) 01950 422295

Doune Marine
Doune, Knoydart
Mallaig PH41 4PV
Tel/Fax (44) 01687 2667

Edinburgh Diving Centre
1 Watson Crescent, Edinburgh
Tel (44) 0131 229 4838
Fax (44) 0131 229 6306

Eyemouth Holiday Park
Fort Road, Eyemouth, Berwickshire
TD14 5ES
Fax (44) 018907 51462
Dive Centre Tel. (44) 018907 51202

Fort William Underwater Centre
Inverness-shire PH33 6LZ
Tel (44) 01397 703786
Fax (44) 01397 704969

Kyle of Lochalsh Dive Centre
Croft Cottage, Kyle of Lochalsh
Tel (44) 01520 722466

Lochaline Dive Centre
Lochaline, Argyll PA34 5XT
Tel/Fax (44) 01967 421662

Oban Divers Ltd.
Glenshellach Road
Oban, Argyllshire PA34 4QJ
Tel (44) 01631 566618
Fax (44) 01631 562755 (tel. first)

Scapa Flow Diving Centre
Burray, Orkney Islands
Tel (44) 01856 73225

Here a large colony of Astacilla longicornis *has attached itself to the stalk of the small bottle-brush hydroid, reflecting the classic case of mimicry for protection from predators.*

The Decompression Stop
5 Hanover Lane, Stranraer
Dumfries & Galloway DG9 7RW
Tel (44) 01776 7170/6260

The Diving Cellar
4 Victoria Street, Stromness, Orkney
Islands
Tel (44) 01856 850055
Fax (44) 01856 850395

The Loch Ness Submarine
Loch Ness, Inverness-shire
Tel (44) 01285 760762

Scoutscroft Diving Centre
Coldingham, Berwickshire
Tel (44) 018907 71338
Fax (44) 018907 71746

Skolla Diving Centre
Gulberwick, Lerwick,
Shetland Islands
Tel (44) 01595 694175

Skye Diving Centre
Harlosh, Dunvegan, Skye
Tel (44) 01470 521366

Splash Sports Services
Unit 8, Market Mews, Market Street
Dundee DD1 3LA
Tel (44) 01382 452828
Fax (44) 0141 339 7788

St. Abbs Dive Centre
Rock House, St. Abbs Harbour,
Berwickshire
Tel (44) 018907 71288

Tobermory Dive Centre
The Haven, Isle of Mull
Tel (44) 01688 302048

Uist Outdoor Centre
Lochmaddy, North Uist,
Outer Hebrides
Tel (44) 01876 500480

Boat Charter

Jean De La Lune
(St. Kilda & Hebrides)
75 Oxgangs Road, Edinburgh
Tel (44) 01501 742514

Kyles of Bute
(Clyde environs)
c/o Andy Lancaster, Kames Hotel
Tighnabruich, Argyll
Tel (44) 01700 811489

M.V. Aquavista
(St. Abbs & Eyemouth)
c/o Alistair Crowe, St. Abbs,
Berwickshire
Tel (44) 018907 71 412

M.V. Heron
(Summer Isles)
Port Cottage, Isle of Tanera Mhor
Achiltibuie,Ullapool IV26 2YN
Tel: (44) 01854 622261
Fax: (44) 01854 622401

M.V. Jean Elaine
(Scapa Flow)
c/o Andy Cuthbertson, 34 Victoria
Street, Stromness, Orkney
Tel/Fax (44) 01856 850 879

M.V. Kylebhan
(Oban & Hebrides)
3 Dal-an-Aiseig, North Connel
Oban, Argyll
Tel (44) 01389 877028

M. V. Monaco
(St.Kilda & Hebrides)
c/o Pointdrake Ltd., Manor Farm,
Chaigley
Tel (44) 01254 826 591

M.V. Ocean Diver
(Clyde environs)
Agnes Patrick Guest House,
Isle of Bute, Clyde
Tel (44) 01374 891145/01274 584451

M.V. Triton
(Scapa Flow)
c/o Steve Mowat, Barkland, Cairston
Road, Stromness, Orkney.
Tel (44) 01856 850624

Macaulay Charters
(Moray Firth)
Harbour Slipways, Inverness
Tel (44) 01463 225398

Minch Charters
(Inner & Outer Hebrides)
Harbour Slipways, Mallaig
Inverness-shire PH41 4QS
Tel (44) 01687 462304
Fax (44) 01687 462378

Technical Diving
(Scapa Flow—Nitrox)
c/o John Thornton, Polrudden
Guest House
Kirkwall, Orkney KW15 1RR
Tel/Fax (44) 01856 874761

This underwater photographer has paused to 'shoot' along one of the many interesting walls to be found all around the coast. ▶

Appendix 2—Emergency Information

IN EMERGENCY Contact H.M. Coastguard Tel 999
Other sources of emergency and services include—
The Scottish Sub Aqua Club
40 Bogmoor Place
Glasgow G51 47Q
Tel 041 425 1021

The British Sub Aqua Club (Scottish Federation)
67 Moredun Park
Gilmerton, Edinburgh
Tel 031 664 4381

Marine Call

Specialist recorded message for all Scottish inshore seas weather forecasting.

Tel: 0891 500 452 Scottish East Coast   Fax: 0336 400 452
Tel: 0891 500 451 Highlands, Orkney
& Shetland   Fax: 0336 400 451
Tel: 0891 500 464 Outer Hebrides   Fax: 0336 400 464
Tel: 0891 500 463 South West Coast   Fax: 0336 400 463

Recompression Chambers

Tel: Aberdeen Royal Infirmary 01224 681818 and ask for Duty Diving Doctor.

Tel: Marine Laboratory Aberdeen 01224 876544

Tel: Fort William Underwater Training Centre 01397 703786.

Tel: Glasgow Western Infirmary 0141 339 8822 and ask for Intensive Care Unit.

Tel: Kyle of Lochalsh, Kishorn Hyperbaric Chamber, Dr. David Murray 01520 733212.

There are also many chambers attached to the North Sea oil industry on ships and oil rigs. In an emergency these may be used by the emergency services involved in any rescue. More often than not, all cases will be referred to Aberdeen.

Bibliography

De Haas & Knorr *Marine Life,* Burke, 1966.

Ferguson, D. *The Wrecks of Scapa Flow,* Kirkwall Press, 1985 (out of print).

George, D. and J. *Marine Life,* Harrap, 1979.

Hamlyn Guide to Seashore and Shallow Seas of Britain & Europe, Hamlyn, 1979.

MacDonald, R. *Dive Scapa Flow,* Mainstream, 1990.

MacDonald, R. *Dive Scotland's Greatest Wrecks,* Mainstream, 1993.

Marine Conservation Society Guide to the Sea Life of Britain & Ireland, Immel, 1988.

McCormick, D. *The Islands of Scotland,* Osprey Publishing, 1974.

Palmer, R. *Undersea Britain,* Immel, 1990.

Picton, B. *Field Guide to Nudibranchs of the British Isles,* Immel, 1994.

Picton, B. *Field Guide to Shallow Water Echinoderms,* Immel, 1993.

Ridley, G. *Dive Scotland,* Volumes 1, 2, & 3, Underwater Publications, 1984/85/92.

Tulloch, B. *Bobby Tulloch's Shetland,* Shetland Times, 1988.

Warman, C. *Guide to St. Abbs & Eyemouth Marine Reserve,* 1987.

Anemonia sulcata *and symbiotic crab.*

Index

Page numbers in boldface indicate photographs.

The end of the day can mean the beginning of an exciting night dive, and there's plenty of great opportunities all around the Scottish coast. Happy and safe diving!

 **Pisces Books®**

Be sure to check out these other great books from Pisces:

Caribbean Reef Ecology
Great Reefs of the World
Skin Diver Magazine's Book of Fishes, 2nd Edition
Shooting Underwater Video: A Complete Guide to the Equipment and Techniques for
    Shooting, Editing, and Post-Production
Snorkeling . . . Here's How
Watching Fishes: Understanding Coral Reef Fish Behavior
Watersports Guide to Cancun

Diving and Snorkeling Guides to:

Australia: Coral Sea and Great Barrier Reef
Australia: Southeast Coast and Tasmania
The Bahamas: Family Islands and Grand
    Bahama
The Bahamas: Nassau and New Providence
    Island, 2nd Ed.
Bali
Belize
The Best Caribbean Diving
Bonaire
The British Virgin Islands
California's Central Coast
The Cayman Islands, 2nd Ed.
Cozumel, 2nd Ed.
Curacao
Fiji
Florida's East Coast, 2nd Ed.
The Florida Keys, 2nd Ed.

The Great Lakes
Guam and Yap
The Hawaiian Islands, 2nd Ed.
Jamaica
Northern California and the Monterey
    Peninsula, 2nd Ed.
The Pacific Northwest
Palau
Puerto Rico
The Red Sea
Roatan and Honduras' Bay Islands
St. Maarten, Saba, and St. Eustatius
Southern California, 2nd Ed.
Texas
Truk Lagoon
The Turks and Caicos Islands
The U.S. Virgin Islands, 2nd Ed.
Vanuatu

Available from your favorite dive shop, bookstore, or directly from the publisher: Pisces
Books®, a division of Gulf Publishing company, Book Division, Dept. AD, P.O. Box 2608,
Houston, Texas 77252-2608. (713) 520-4444.

Include purchase price plus $4.95 for shipping and handling. IL, NJ, PA, and TX residents add appropriate tax.